Hope for the Future

Hope for the Future

Answering God's Call to Justice for Our Children

Shannon Daley-Harris

WJK WESTMINSTER
JOHN KNOX PRESS
LOUISVILLE · KENTUCKY

Unless otherwise indicated, Scripture quotations are from the New Revised Standard Version of the Bible, copyright © 1989 by the Division of Christian Education of the National Council of the Churches of Christ in the U.S.A., and are used by permission.

Scripture quotations marked CEB are from the Common English Bible, © 2011 Common English Bible.

Excerpt from *The Irresistible Revolution: Living as an Ordinary Radical* by Shane Claiborne Copyright © 2006 by The Simple Way. Used by permission of Zondervan. www.zondervan.com. Excerpt from Gary Bellow's address to the Alliance of Justice Luncheon in 1996 used by permission of the estate of Gary Bellow. Excerpts from the website of the Children's Defense Fund are used by permission; courtesy of the Children's Defense Fund.

Book design by Sharon Adams
Cover design by Barbara LeVan Fisher / levanfisherstudio.com

Library of Congress Cataloging-in-Publication Data
Names: Daley-Harris, Shannon, author.
Title: Hope for the future : answering God's call to justice for our children / Shannon Daley-Harris.
Description: First edition. | Louisville, Kentucky : Westminster John Knox Press, [2016] | Includes bibliographical references.
Identifiers: LCCN 2016018710 (print) | LCCN 2016031880 (ebook) | ISBN 9780664261634 (pbk. : alk. paper) | ISBN 9781611648089 (ebk.)
Subjects: LCSH: Children—Religious aspects—Christianity. | Children in the Bible. | Children—Biblical teaching. | Bible. Old Testament—Criticism, interpretation, etc. | Church work with children.
Classification: LCC BT705 .D35 2016 (print) | LCC BT705 (ebook) | DDC 252—dc23
LC record available at https://lccn.loc.gov/2016018710

Most Westminster John Knox Press books are available at special quantity discounts when purchased in bulk by corporations, organizations, and special-interest groups. For more information, please e-mail SpecialSales@wjkbooks.com.

For Micah and Sophie
and for all children—beloved by God, entrusted to our care

Thus says the LORD:
  A voice is heard in Ramah,
    lamentation and bitter weeping.
  Rachel is weeping for her children;
    she refuses to be comforted for her children,
    because they are no more.
Thus says the LORD:
  Keep your voice from weeping,
    and your eyes from tears;
  for there is a reward for your work,
              says the LORD:
    they shall come back from the land of the enemy;
  there is hope for your future,
              says the LORD:
    your children shall come back to their own country.
                                        (Jer. 31:15–17)

Contents

Foreword by Marian Wright Edelman   ix
Preface   xiii
Acknowledgments   xix

Part I: Called
1. From Weeping to Work (*Jeremiah 31*)   3
2. Singing a New Song (*Psalm 33*)   13
3. Stumbling Blocks and Cornerstones (*Isaiah 28*)   25
4. Troops, Trumpets, and Torches (*Judges 7*)   35

Part II: Challenged
5. What's Next? (*Jonah*)   49
6. Team of Rivals (*Isaiah 11*)   59
7. Certainly Not (*Acts 16*)   67
8. Confusion in the Valley of Vision (*Isaiah 22*)   79

Part III: Sustained
9. Parables of Persistence (*Luke 18*)   93
10. Vigilance (*Hebrews 10*)   107
11. Shepherd for the Lost (*Matthew 18*)   117
12. Godspeed (*Deuteronomy 16*)   127

Resources for Faithful Child Advocacy from the
    Children's Defense Fund   135
Notes   139

Foreword

I am a child of the church. From my earliest days, there was never a separation between the church and the calling to care for and seek justice for children. My daddy was a Baptist preacher (as was his father and, later, my brother Harry). My mother welcomed countless children into our home, providing whatever was needed, whether it was a pair of shoes or a safe place to stay. Together, my parents and the other adults in the church preached and lived a message that each of us was a beloved and precious child of God—bulwark against the racism of our segregated Southern town. There was no division between what was preached on Sunday and proclaimed during the week, between the worship on Sunday and the weekday work to care for and speak up for those who were poor, elderly, young, or vulnerable.

Of the countless gifts my parents gave me, the enduring sense of God's call to child advocacy has shaped my life and every breath. We cannot claim to be followers of Jesus, the most famous poor child in history, if we do not see Christ in the face of every poor child today and respond with faithful acts of compassion and justice.

When we look at any of the great social movements for systemic justice in our nation—from the abolition of slavery to the end of child labor to civil rights—the faith community was at the forefront (although in each instance there was also a segment of the religious community that worked against those just causes). We will not create the change we need to make America just for children without the leadership and involvement of the faith community. And so children—especially the poorest and most vulnerable—need the work and witness of the faith community. At the same time, I believe that without seeking justice for children, the faith community can't fulfill its calling and charge from Jesus who said, "Whoever welcomes one such child in my name welcomes me," and the prophets who proclaimed that what God requires of us is to do justice and love kindness and walk humbly with God. And so the faith community needs the work and witness of child advocacy for its own sake, to live most fully its faith.

From its inception, the Children's Defense Fund has worked with people like you who want to connect their faith with their concern for children and respond to God's call to love, protect, and seek justice for children. For more than a quarter century, Shannon Daley-Harris has guided CDF's partnership with the faith community as we have engaged faithful individuals, places of worship, denominations, and organizations across the religious spectrum to raise a strong and effective voice for the children of our nation. Shannon launched the National Observance of Children's Sabbath in 1992 to coalesce the diverse voices of religious organizations and denominations into a united call for justice on behalf of children—a call that is raised each October and reverberates through ongoing efforts throughout the year.

In 1995, Shannon launched CDF's Samuel DeWitt Proctor Institute for Child Advocacy Ministry held at CDF Haley Farm each July. There, hundreds of clergy, Christian educators, young adults, child advocates, and those serving children directly gather for inspiring preaching, insightful teaching, empowering workshops, and sustaining connections. This intergenerational, interracial, ecumenical gathering is a profound experience of Beloved Community as we seek the vision, information, strategies, and sustenance to continue building a mighty movement for justice for children.

Shannon began an annual tradition of a January women's spiritual retreat in 1997. Many of the meditations in this collection that you are about to read were first preached at one of those annual gatherings of a few dozen women leaders. I hope that you will be inspired and sustained by them as we were and that you will hear afresh God's call to put your faith into action, God's promise of strength to meet the challenges, and God's promise of presence to sustain you.

We have so much work to do to make our world safe for children. We don't have a minute to wait or a child to waste. CDF's logo is a child's drawing of the fisherman's prayer, "Dear Lord, be good to me. The sea is so wide, and my boat is so small." Our children are overwhelmed by an ocean of troubles—rising poverty, gun violence, abuse and neglect, and so much more that threatens to drown them. The chapel at CDF Haley Farm—where so many of these meditations were first preached—is shaped like an ark. Our calling is to provide a safe ark of protection for our children and to work against the floodwaters of poverty and other harm. We are God's hands and feet and voices here on earth, and we need to answer that child's prayer by doing all we can to rescue our children—*God's* beloved children. May you find hope, courage, and persistence to answer that call.

In hope and faith—

Marian Wright Edelman
Epiphany 2016

Preface

Most of us, whether in the pew or in the pulpit, have heard young ones sing, "Jesus loves the little children, all the children of the world." We've read well-worn pages of Scripture that urge us to "suffer the little ones" and remind us what God requires of us: to do justice, to love kindness, and to walk humbly with God. We have, for the most part, seen the children of our congregations loved, nurtured, blessed.

Yet many of us, in our lives beyond the church, are aware of children who are not welcomed, who are not loved and protected, who don't experience kindness and justice. Whether they are the children whose lives we touch through our professional or volunteer work, the children for whom we advocate, or the children that we hear about in the news, we recognize that many children *don't* experience the love and justice God intends for each and every one. And so we yearn for more inspiration, more guidance, more sustenance from our faith so that we can begin to close this gap between the world God intends and the one we know, between our Sunday worship and our weekday work for children who suffer injustice.

What is God's word to us in the tension between the vision and the reality? What resources can we draw on in Scripture, story, and statistic? What lessons can we learn from biblical times, historic movements for justice, and our own day? Theologian Karl

Barth is said to have instructed us to read with the Bible in one hand and newspaper in the other. The meditations in this book invite you to go further—as you read, hold not only the Bible and newspaper but also children on your lap, figuratively, as well as the reports that document the crises confronting our nation's children, history books chronicling earlier movements for justice, and photographs of unsung heroes who made a difference.

The four meditations in part 1, "Called," invite us to listen for how God is calling us to love and seek justice for children. Can we hear the charge to move from weeping to work to restore our children to community? What "new song" are we called to sing that will build a movement for change? How will we respond to the call to remove stumbling blocks of poverty, violence, and other forms of injustice and replace them with a cornerstone for which justice is the measure? Do we believe that the few of us can rout mighty forces of oppression? How can we organize to answer that call and then call others to join us?

The four meditations in part 2, "Challenged," offer perspectives on facing the difficulties in this calling of faithful child advocacy. Will we answer God's call to the next challenging mission even if it seems too huge, hostile, hopeless, or hard? Can we envision a day when opponents work together, when you can lose and still win? How do we decide when to compromise and when to stand firm for the justice our children deserve? Will we abandon our responsibilities in the face of chaos and challenge, or will we live into the vision of a community that protects its children? What does it look like when we hold before us a clear vision of what God intends—communities working together for the sake of every child, not just "their own"?

Draw on the final four meditations in part 3, "Sustained," to keep yourself going as you love, protect, and seek justice for children. We need persistence to keep at this calling of child advocacy. Draw inspiration from parables of persistence in Scripture, history, and our own day. We cannot shrink back; hear words of comfort and courage to press ahead and vigilantly ensure that our children are safe from harm. Knowing that every single child matters to God can keep us going even when we are discouraged;

the examples of those who embody the tenacious love of the Good Shepherd can inspire us not to give up and to leave no child behind. Finally, we are sent to pursue justice with urgency and persistence, recalling that "Godspeed" is a prayer that God will speed us on our way for a successful journey until we—and all children—are safely home.

Each of these meditations originated as a sermon prepared for and preached to a particular community. One was preached from the pulpit to a large, multiethnic urban congregation on the National Observance of Children's Sabbath weekend; another was delivered in a small seminary chapel for Children's Sabbath. Many were preached at the annual women's spiritual retreat at CDF Haley Farm, offered while seated in a circle alongside a few dozen women leaders, many of whom came up through the civil rights movement and all of whom have devoted their lives to justice and working for children. In every instance, these meditations were preached to those who are not only "hearers of the word" but also "doers of the word." Those who first heard these words didn't need to be convinced to care about children facing an ocean of troubles—they already did. No, what those hearers and longtime doers yearned for was fresh inspiration, another perspective on facing challenges, a deeper drink of the sustenance that faith can provide for this journey toward justice.

I believe the same is true for you. It is why you hold this book in your hands: you already care deeply about the problems so many children face; you may already have worked long and faithfully to improve the lives of children; and you long for a fresh word from God to help you make a difference. My hope and prayer is that for you, too, these meditations will be inspiration, affirmation, and sustenance as you seek to continue to be a doer of God's word and to move from weeping to the work that will help usher in the return of all our children to safety.

Questions for Faithful Response are offered after each meditation. Perhaps you will use them as you prepare for your own preaching. Or they may deepen your devotional time. You can use them in a Bible study discussion or as a prompt for conversation in a social action committee meeting or gathering of parents or youths. As there are twelve meditations, you may want to read one each month in a group setting. Or you may want to turn to one that speaks to where you are in your own walk, work, and witness—whether your personal need is for motivation or guidance or encouragement. Most of all, I hope that they are an encouragement and resource so that you draw on what is on the page and in your heart to move into ever more faithful, active response to improve the lives of children through courageous advocacy and compassionate service.

The last question in each of the Questions for Faithful Response is framed for parents and any who are caring for children—such as grandparents and other relatives and teachers in classroom or congregation. Children are not merely the recipients of our advocacy, action, and care; they are also powerful agents of change themselves. Children have deep wells of concern, strong compasses for what is just and moral, boundless energy, a sense of urgency, and enthusiasm for action. While the meditations themselves are not written for children, use the last question in each set as a jumping-off point for a conversation with a child or children in your life, and look for faithful ways to act together to improve the lives of children with love and justice.

More than twenty years ago, as I wrote what would be the first-ever interfaith worship service at the Children's Defense Fund's annual national conference, I drew on the words in Jeremiah to the grieving parent, Rachel, who wept over the loss of her children:

> Thus says the LORD:
> Keep your voice from weeping
>   and your eyes from tears;
> for there is a reward for your work,
>
>   says the LORD:
>   they shall come back from the land of the enemy;
> there is hope for your future,
>
>   says the LORD:
>   your children shall come back to their own country.
>   (Jer. 31:16–17)

Even in the midst of the enormous problems our children face—poverty, gun violence, abuse, neglect, lack of health care, and more—I do believe there is hope for our future, that we can bring all children to an experience of safety, love, and justice. It will take more than weeping, God reminds us, it will take work—and to keep at that work we need to stay close to God. May these meditations offer you anew the inspiration of God's calling, God's guidance for the challenges you encounter, and sustenance to continue to pursue justice with urgency, persistence, and faith.

Acknowledgments

I am profoundly grateful to Marian Wright Edelman, CDF's founder and president, who has inspired me with her vision, commitment, and life of putting faith into action for children. It is a blessing to serve this cause with her leadership and extraordinary example. CDF is made up of incredibly dedicated staff members past and present; their teamwork to build the movement for children makes it impossible to single out just a few, but I trust they know that I count myself incredibly lucky to be partners with them in this work.

My deep thanks also to the extraordinary faculty-in-residence of CDF's Samuel DeWitt Proctor Institute for Child Advocacy Ministry for their generosity, prophetic and pastoral ministry, and the gift of serving alongside and learning from them: the late Dr. Fred Craddock, Rev. Will Gipson, Dr. Don Lewis, Dr. Otis Moss Jr., Dr. Otis Moss III, the late Dr. Samuel DeWitt Proctor, Dr. Frederick J. Streets, Dr. Eli Wilson, and Dr. Janet Wolf. The longest serving faculty-in-residence at Proctor, Dr. Eileen W. Lindner, has been a mentor and friend in ministry from my earliest days at CDF, and I learned first from her the power of story in preaching; I owe her a special debt of thanks.

I've been blessed to worship in the black church tradition over the past twenty-six years, and one of the many gifts has been experiencing preaching as a collaboration between preacher and congregation, with the congregation's engagement and response an inextricable part of the sermon. These meditations wouldn't exist without the generous response, engagement, and witness of the community of (mostly) women for whom and with whom they came to be, and so to them I owe deep gratitude.

I am grateful to Dr. Jacq Lapsley, associate professor of Old Testament at Princeton Theological Seminary, for her generous and knowledgeable feedback on this manuscript. Any errors that remain are, of course, mine. Thanks also to Carol Wehrheim for her thoughtful review of the Questions for Faithful Response.

Working with the tremendous Westminster John Knox team has been wonderful, and this book has benefited greatly from the editorial insights of Jessica Miller Kelley and David Dobson, Frances Purifoy's careful copyediting, and Kerri Daly's work to spread the word and get it into many hands. My thanks to Julie Tonini for her patience, support, and guidance as she shepherded the book through production.

My parents, the Revs. Patti and Eliot Daley, are both Presbyterian clergy and child advocates in their own ways. I am grateful for their lifelong example of ministering—with and without the collar—to improve the lives of children and for their love of the Word and words that have shaped my life and are reflected in this book. I am blessed to be their child.

My husband, Sam, has been a sounding board and champion as I wrote this book and throughout our two decades of marriage. I am profoundly grateful for the bedrock of his love and support.

Micah and Sophie are the greatest blessing and joy of my life. They remind me every day of the preciousness of every child's life and fuel my determination to work so that *every* child has the love, protection, and opportunities to live in the fullness of life that God intends.

Part I

Called

Chapter One

From Weeping to Work

Jeremiah 31

Thus says the LORD:
A voice is heard in Ramah,
  lamentation and bitter weeping.
Rachel is weeping for her children;
  she refuses to be comforted for her children,
  because they are no more.
Thus says the LORD:
Keep your voice from weeping
  and your eyes from tears;
for there is a reward for your work,
                              says the LORD:
  they shall come back from the land of the enemy;
there is hope for your future,
                              says the LORD:
  your children shall come back to their own country.
                              (Jer. 31:15–17)

It was a beautiful October morning, and I stood in line at the neighborhood Starbucks, thinking about my half-caf, iced, venti, skim, two-pump, no-whip mocha. The line was long and moved slowly as the baristas made other people's equally high-maintenance

3

orders, so I picked up a copy of the *New York Times* and began to read. I read, that is, until the print began to swim in front of my tear-filled eyes. This is as far as I got:

> Kete Krachi, Ghana—Just before 5 a.m., with the sky still dark over Lake Volta, Mark Kwadwo was roused from his spot on the damp dirt floor. It was time for work.
>
> Shivering in the predawn chill, he helped paddle a canoe a mile out from shore. For five more hours, as his co-workers yanked up a fishing net, Mark bailed water to keep the canoe from swamping.
>
> He had last eaten the day before. His broken wooden paddle was so heavy he could barely lift it. But he raptly followed each command from Kwadwo Takyi, the powerfully built 31-year-old in the back of the canoe who freely deals out beatings.
>
> Mark Kwadwo is 6 years old. About 30 pounds, dressed in a pair of blue and red underpants and a Little Mermaid T-shirt, he looks more like an oversized toddler than a boat hand.
>
> He is too young to understand why he has ended up in this fishing village, a two-day trek from his home.
>
> But the three older boys who work with him know why. Like Mark, they are indentured servants, leased by their impoverished parents to Takyi for as little as $20 a year.[1]

Weeping

I stood there in line at the Starbucks weeping, overcome by such a painful sense of despair and helplessness at changing the child's circumstances, at bringing him home to his family, that I could read no more.

I wasn't the only one who wept over Mark Kwadwo. The *New York Times* got many letters in response to the article, including this one from a teacher. She wrote, in part,

There are moments when there is value in simply feeling the deep pain of another's situation. But in an age when most of us . . . already feel powerless about what happens in the world, a little bit of guidance toward action—anything to hang on to—would have been both kind and potentially helpful for all.[2]

Have you ever felt that way? That you cannot bear to let yourself feel another's pain when you feel helpless to ease it?

It is not just the suffering of a six-year-old half a world away that is cause for weeping and lament today. Here, even here in our nation, 14.5 million children live in poverty and suffer undeserved deprivation and limitations and obstacles.[3]

Here, even here, nearly 3.9 million children don't have health coverage and may not be able to see a doctor when needed.[4]

Here, even here, children—especially black and Latino boys—are being pushed along a cradle-to-prison pipeline so that a black boy still in elementary school today faces a one-in-three risk of incarceration in his lifetime.[5]

Here, yes, even here, there are children facing enormous odds against them—poverty and violence and lost childhood—with only their faith and their families to cling to. Children like eight-year-old Gail, who was asked to write an essay about her Chicago neighborhood for a contest sponsored by a bank. The bank had expected to receive essays telling of friendly postmen and games of hopscotch; instead they received essays like this one from Gail:

> In my neighborhood there is a lot of shooting and three people got shot. On the next day when I was going to school I saw a little stream of blood on the ground. One day after school me and my mother had to dodge bullets—I was not scared. There is a church and a school that I go to in my neighborhood. There are a lot of stores in my neighborhood also. There are robbers that live in my building, they broke into our house twice. There are rowhouses in

my neighborhood and a man got shot and he was dead. By
King High School Susan Harris got shot and she died. It
was in the newspaper. When me and my mother was going
to church we could see the fire from the guns being shot in
4414 building. I was not scared. In my neighborhood there
are too many fights. I have never been in a fight before.
There are many trees in my neighborhood. God is going to
come back one day and judge the whole world. Not just my
neighborhood. I know these are really, really bad things, but
I have some good things in my neighborhood. Like sometimes my neighborhood is peaceful and quiet and there is no
shooting. When me and my mother and some of my friends
go to the lake we have a lot of fun. Sometimes the children in
my building go to Sunday School with me and my mother.
Also the building I live in is so tall I can see downtown and
the lake. It looks so pretty. I believe in God and I know one
day we will be in a gooder place than we are now.[6]

Sometimes the stories are so sad and the pain is so great that
we turn away. Have you ever felt that way? Sometimes the numbers are simply numbing, and we can't even cry. Have you ever
felt that way? And then sometimes we let ourselves feel that pain
and let our hearts weep. Have you ever felt that way? God has
and God knows; the God who became incarnate and suffered the
depths of human pain hears us and weeps with us and with our
children.

From Weeping to Work

Yet that God of compassion is also a God of action and a God
of justice, and so it is not enough merely to sit dissolved in compassionate tears. "Keep your voice from weeping and your eyes
from tears," says our God. "There is a reward for your work"
(Jer. 31:16).

While God hears our grief and pain at circumstances of injustice that demand change, God's response is to call on God's people to create the change that is needed. It is not enough to cry out

and be heard. Rachel is told that the change will come as a reward for her *work.*

For her work? For our work? Yes, we are called to work: the real work of restoring justice, returning to covenant community that protects the children, those who are poor, and the strangers, loving our God with all our heart and mind and strength and our neighbors as ourselves—our neighbors like Mark in Ghana, our neighbors like Gail in Chicago, our neighbors even in our own communities.

The Women's Bible Commentary reflects on the "return" that God promises as a reward for our work:

> The transformed society imagined in these poems provides a social vision that includes everyone not only in worship but also at the banquet of material life. . . . The society will satisfy the basic human needs of all, and it will be characterized by justice, harmony, and peace. . . . The comforting of Rachel, mother of Israel, symbolizes that new society.[7]

The hopeful future that is promised, for which we must work, is one in which justice is restored, compassion is practiced, and the community has rededicated itself to living in right relationship with God and with one another.

There Is Hope for Your Future; Your Children Shall Come Back

We are summoned out of grief to this work with a promise to sustain us in that difficult calling. The promise isn't vague or otherworldly—it's not the "gooder place" that Gail believes is her only hope. No, God's promise is embodied in the very real well-being and restoration of our children. The promise to Rachel is that the children will come back to their own country; *that* is the "hope for your future."

There is hope for your future, says our God. True, 14.5 million children in our rich nation are living in poverty, but we know what to do to bring a better tomorrow. Children can't move out of poverty on their own, but there are effective ways that we as a nation can lift children and their families out of poverty or at least protect them from poverty's worst effects. We know what works. Programs that reduce poverty by providing cash or near-cash assistance—such as the Supplemental Nutrition Assistance Program (SNAP, commonly known as food stamps), the Temporary Assistance for Needy Families Program (commonly called welfare), and the Earned Income Tax Credit—can ease the worst effects of poverty for millions of children. Government safety-net programs lifted nine million children from poverty in 2012. Child poverty would have been 57 percent higher without government tax credits and food, housing, and energy benefits, and extreme poverty would have been 240 percent higher.[8] Still, *no* child deserves to live in poverty, so there is more work to be done so that every family has the job training, living wage, health care, child care, and other supports they need to keep children out of poverty and ready to thrive.

There is hope for your future, says our God. Some 3.9 million children may lack health coverage today, but we have the real opportunity to ensure that every child in our nation has health coverage if we join our voices to demand justice through affordable, available coverage and reach out to ensure that families get enrolled in the coverage that is available. There's no mystery: children need regular health care for their developing minds and bodies. They need timely treatment for illness and injury. It will save our nation money in the long run, but more importantly it will save lives and is the right thing to do. Imagine the better tomorrow when every child has the benefit of health coverage and a shot at good health.

There is hope for your future, says our God. It is true that a black boy born in 2001 faces a one-in-three risk of imprisonment in his lifetime, but we can *change* the odds. We can work to provide a better tomorrow for boys of color and for us all. What is currently painting such a grim picture for young boys of color, pushing them along the pipeline to prison? Poverty, racism, lack of health and mental-health care, abuse and neglect, failing schools, dangerous neighborhoods. But we know how to address and solve those problems; we know what works. CDF Freedom Schools® sites have welcomed children who might have traveled through the pipeline to prison, touching the lives of more than 137,000 pre-K-12 children since 1995, and more than sixteen thousand college students and recent graduates have been trained by CDF to deliver this empowering model with reading and other enrichment, parent involvement, and community-building skills and experiences.[9] Head Start programs have demonstrated that investing in early childhood development saves us financial and human costs, as Head Start graduates do better in school and are more likely to stay out of trouble. Innovative schools have shown how high expectations, excellent teaching, and comprehensive support can fill graduation stages instead of prison cells with black, Latino, poor, and at-risk students. Even something as simple as mentoring a young person as a Big Brother or Big Sister can transform his or her life . . . and ours, too.

There is hope for your future, says our God. Your children shall return to their own country. As for Mark Kwadwo, the six-year-old boat hand in Ghana—someone read about his story and didn't just weep but got to work. In Missouri, Pam and Randy Cope read the *New York Times* story about Mark and wanted to help. The parents of four had suffered a devastating loss when their fifteen-year-old son, Jantsen, died suddenly from an undetected heart defect in 1999. After weeping, they got to work. In Jantsen's memory, Pam and Randy launched Touch a Life Ministries, an organization helping children in dire situations in Cambodia, Vietnam, Nicaragua, and elsewhere. "Their grief—and hope—have led them on a journey to try to care for hurting children of the world," said Randy's brother, the Rev. Mike Cope.[10]

After learning of Mark Kwadwo's plight, Pam teamed up with a small nonprofit in Ghana, Pacodep, run by a Kete Krachi school teacher and a Dutch volunteer. Together, they rescued not only Mark but the other children indentured to the same master, "paying for new nets, boat repairs, and other needs in exchange for the children's freedom." The freed children, whose destitute parents could not provide for them at home, now enjoy the security of shelter, meals, schooling, and recreation in a Christian-run orphanage.[11]

A staff member who works at the orphanage prays for the children still in bondage—and for their masters. "For slavery to end, the people who exploit children also must be changed, the missionary said. 'There are many more children,' he said, 'and God is working through a lot of people to show us what to do next.'"[12]

The name of Mark's new school? The Village of Hope. *There is hope for your future, says our God.* We are called by the God of hope to embody a village, nation, and world of hope. We are called to this ministry by God, who created every child in God's own image. We are called to this ministry by Jesus, who told us that whenever we welcome one such child in his name we welcome him and not only him but the one who sent him. We are sustained in this ministry by the Holy Spirit, the Advocate, who calls us into community and sends us out to work for justice.

There is hope for your future. You, whose voice God has heard weeping: How will you make your voice heard as you call for justice and for change? You, whose eyes have been full of tears: What new opportunities for action do you see before you? You who have wept for the suffering of children: What is the work you are called to do? You who have lamented the children who are lost: What is the hope for their future that will sustain you?

A voice is heard in Ramah, in Washington, in your community: What will you proclaim?

∼

Questions for Faithful Response

1. Who are the children for whom you weep?

2. When have you felt so much sadness, pain, or numbness at the suffering of children that you have turned away? When have you let yourself feel that pain at children's suffering? What has made the difference between the two experiences?

3. God's promise is embodied in the very real well-being and restoration of our children. The promise to Rachel is that the children will come back to their own country; *that* is the "hope for your future." Close your eyes and envision what the promise of children restored to their community would look like for us in our day. What does "hope for your future" look like to you?

4. Rachel is told that change will come as a reward for her *work*. "There are many more children," the Village of Hope worker said, "and God is working through a lot of people to show us what to do next." What work do you feel you are being led to do next? How will you make your voice heard as you call for justice and for change? What new opportunities for action do you see before you?

5. *For parents and other caregivers:* Often our desire is to shield our children from news stories or information that would make them sad or anxious, especially when it concerns other children. Children have a natural wellspring of empathy. How have or how could you connect your child's empathy with real problems facing other children in a way that is empowering, hopeful, and helpful?

Chapter Two

Singing a New Song

Psalm 33

All you who are righteous,
    shout joyfully to the Lord!
It's right for those who do right to praise God.
Give thanks to the Lord with the lyre!
    Sing praises to [God] with the ten-stringed harp!
Sing to [God] a new song!
    Play your best with joyful shouts!
Because the Lord's word is right,
    [God's] every act is done in good faith.
[God] loves righteousness and justice;
    the Lord's faithful love fills the whole earth.
"The skies were made by the Lord's word,
    all their starry multitude by the breath of [God's] mouth.
[God] gathered the ocean waters into a heap;
    [God] put the deep seas into storerooms.
All the earth honors the Lord;
    all the earth's inhabitants stand in awe of [God].
Because when [God] spoke, it happened!
    When [God] commanded, there it was!

The LORD overrules what the nations plan;
> [God] frustrates what the peoples intend to do.

But the LORD's plan stands forever;
> what [God] intends to do lasts from one generation to
> the next.

The nation whose God is the LORD,
> the people whom God has chosen as [God's] possession,
> is truly happy!

The LORD looks down from heaven;
> [God] sees every human being.

From [God's] dwelling place God observes all who live
on earth.

> God is the one who made all their hearts,
the one who knows everything they do.

Kings aren't saved by the strength of their armies;
> warriors aren't rescued by how much power they have.

A warhorse is a bad bet for victory;
> it can't save despite its great strength.

But look here: the LORD's eyes watch all who honor [God],
> all who wait for [God's] faithful love,
> to deliver their lives from death
> and keep them alive during a famine.

We put our hope in the LORD.
> [God] is our help and our shield.

Our heart rejoices in God
> because we trust [God's] holy name.

LORD, let your faithful love surround us
> because we wait for you.

(Ps. 33 CEB)

Singing a New Song

Some time ago, as I was flipping through TV channels, I came across the movie *Invictus*, featuring Morgan Freeman as Nelson Mandela and Matt Damon as Francois Pinaar, the captain of the white Afrikaaner rugby team the Springboks. Do you remember that incredible true story of how President Mandela supported the rugby team—which had been a hated symbol of white privilege and exclusion? White and black South Africans were transformed by President Mandela's embrace of the team—a small but critical step forward in the slow, difficult work of forging a new, united, more just nation.

The movie depicts their first encounter. President Mandela has invited the rugby captain to come to tea. As they discuss the challenges of their respective jobs, President Mandela and Francois agree that getting people to do their best, especially when playing for the nation's team, is not so difficult. President Mandela then muses about the difficulty of getting people to do *better* than their best, better than they have ever imagined they could be.

Leading by example is part of it, President Mandela acknowledges, but he then adds that it takes even more than that—it requires inspiration. "How do we inspire ourselves to greatness, when nothing less will do? How do we inspire everyone around us?" he asks. Pondering, President Mandela observes that the work of others sometimes provides that inspiration. He says that he draws inspiration from a poem, "Invictus." Francois chimes in, describing the tension-laden silence of the bus ride when the team is headed for a big match. When he feels the moment is right, he tells President Mandela, he asks the bus driver to play a particular song. As the team listens together to that song, they gain confidence and courage to face the challenge that lies ahead.

President Mandela responds enthusiastically, recalling the 1992 Olympic Games in Barcelona. "The whole stadium welcomed me with a song. At the time the future—our future—seemed very bleak. But to hear that song, in voices from all over our planet . . . it made me very proud to be South African. It helped me to come home and do better. It allowed me to expect more of myself." Francois asks which song it was; President Mandela tells him it was *Nkosi Sikelel' iAfrika* (God Bless Africa.) "A very inspiring song. . . . We need inspiration, Francois. . . . Because, in order to build our nation, we all need to exceed our own expectations."[1]

Days That Are Bleak

This is a time, as it was for President Mandela, when it can feel as though our future is bleak. The Children's Defense Fund documents what many of us know from experience: children across our nation face challenges, and for children in poverty and even more so for black children, the odds are stacked especially high against them. CDF reports that the following occur for black children each day in America:

- 3 children or teens are killed by guns.
- 4 children or teens die from accidents.
- 148 babies are born without health insurance.
- 329 babies are born into extreme poverty.
- 318 public school students are corporally punished.*
- 399 children are confirmed as abused or neglected.
- 603 babies are born into poverty.
- 763 high school students drop out.*
- 1,174 children are arrested.
- 4,529 public school students are suspended.*[2]

Yes, it can feel like our children's future, our future, is bleak. We need a new song. Not a song set to music, per se, but a new song—metaphorically—that will unite, inspire, and encourage us to exceed our expectations to build a nation fit for our children even when, especially when, the future looks bleak.

Looking at the Psalm

The new song that the psalmist summons us to join affirms God's sovereign love, justice, and power. The psalm has as many lines as there are letters of the Hebrew alphabet, symbolizing the completeness of God's sovereignty. The psalmist affirms that there is no realm of life that is beyond the reach of God: creation, nations and peoples, humanity in general, the faithful in particular . . . *all* of our lives spring from the word, work, and will of God.[3]

The new song that the psalmist would have us proclaim tells the truth belying popular perception: strength doesn't lie in political powers or armies but in the steadfast love and justice of God. A new song is a vision, an anticipation, a proclamation of God's priorities and God's promise of victory.

The psalmist's new song reminds us that the plans of nations and people are no match for the will of God. God's love and justice is our ultimate hope and our help—surely a cause for rejoicing, a source of strength and inspiration for our own words and work.

The new song that the psalmist urges isn't a solo. The Hebrew imperatives in the first three verses are in the plural form: the psalmist is saying, "*All* of you" shout joyfully, give thanks, sing praises, sing a new song, and play your best.

What is the "new song" we will sing through our work and our witness, our organizing and our advocacy, our preaching and our protests that will declare and help to usher in God's righteousness, justice, and love?

"*Sing to God a new song! Play your best with joyful shouts! God loves righteousness and justice; God's faithful love fills the whole earth.*"

Inspiration to Exceed Our Own Expectations

In 1951, sixteen-year-old Barbara Rose Johns looked at her segregated high school, Robert R. Moton High School in Farmville, Virginia, and the future looked bleak. But as she tried something new, she exceeded even her own expectations. Here is how her younger sister Joan remembers it:

> The school was for black students only. There was a white school in Farmville. We had separate facilities and most of the school supplies we got were torn and tattered, and we didn't have enough supplies to write with. The school we went to was overcrowded. Consequently, the county decided to build three tarpaper shacks for us to hold classes in. . . . In winter the school was very cold. . . . When it rained we would get water through the ceiling. So there were lots of

pails sitting around the classroom. And sometimes we had to raise our umbrellas to keep the water off our heads. It was a very difficult setting for trying to learn.

And I remember we were always talking about how bad the conditions were but we didn't know what to do about it. So one day my sister and a group of students that she chose decided to do something about it.

There was a music teacher by the name of Inez Davenport that Barbara confided in. When [Barbara] discussed the conditions of the school with Miss Davenport, Miss Davenport said to her, finally, "Why don't you do something about it?" With that . . . [Barbara] tried to come up with a plan of what she could do to get a better school.[4]

Although Joan saw her sister as an introvert, a serious student who "stayed to herself," Barbara reached out to four classmates, and together they developed a plan for the students to go on strike. Barbara's sister and the other students were unaware of the plan when they were called to the auditorium for a school assembly. To Joan's astonishment, when the auditorium curtain was raised, it revealed not the expected principal but instead her sister. Joan recalls:

I was totally shocked. [Barbara] walked up to the podium, and she started to tell everyone that she wanted us to cooperate with her because the school was going out on a strike. I remember sitting in my seat and trying to go as low in the seat as I possibly could because I knew that what she was doing was going to have severe consequences. I didn't know what they were going to be, but I knew that there were going to be some. She stood up there and addressed the school. She seemed to have everyone's attention. . . . At one point, she took off her shoe, and she banged on the podium and said we were going to go out on strike and would everyone please cooperate and "Don't be afraid, just follow us out." So we did. The entire student body followed her out.[5]

The students stayed out of school the following days and instead met at the First Baptist Church to plan what they would do next to build the movement. Barbara telephoned two lawyers from Richmond, Virginia, Spotswood Robinson and Oliver Hill, to ask for their help. Neither of the busy lawyers responded to her first calls. Joan remembers, "However, Mr. Oliver Hill would tell me later that he got a call from Barbara and she was very persistent. She told him that we needed him and that he just had to come. . . . He said that she said to him, 'You must come and help us.' He said she just kept calling him until he decided to take the case."

Spotswood Robinson and Oliver Hill filed suit at the federal courthouse using the Moton High School case to end segregated schools in Virginia. They lost, but in their appeal the lawyers incorporated the Moton case with three other similar suits that became known as Brown v. Board of Education.

Looking back, Joan says, "I don't believe Barbara knew anything about the fact that [her walk-out] would change the course of history. However, I remember her being so excited and shouting about it when the decision came down and we heard about it. . . . I don't think she knew that what she and the other students did would have any kind of impact on the nation that resulted in the Brown v. Board of Education case."[6]

With the encouragement of her music teacher, when the future looked bleak, Barbara led the school in a new song of activism that helped them exceed even their own expectations and changed the course of history.

"Sing to God a new song! Play your best with joyful shouts! God loves righteousness and justice; God's faithful love fills the whole earth."

Song Leaders

The "new song" that we are called to sing through our words and work and witness is one that engages the community in its creation. That's something Bernice Johnson Reagon of the musical group Sweet Honey in the Rock knows. Here's how she described her experience of song in the civil rights movement. Listen for what it has to say to us today as we think about our own movement for children. In *Eyes on the Prize*, Bernice recalled, "I [was] arrested in the second wave of arrests in Albany, [Georgia]. And when we got to jail, Slater King, who was already in jail, said, 'Bernice, is that you?' And I said yes. And he said, 'Sing a song.'"[7]

Bernice explains, "The singing tradition in Albany was congregational. There were no soloists; there were song leaders. If Slater said, 'Bernice, sing a song,' he wasn't asking for a solo; he was asking me to plant a seed. The minute you start the song, the song is created by everybody there. There is really almost a musical explosion."[8]

This new song that we are called to sing—to build the momentum for the children's movement, for organizing in our congregations and communities and networks—is about leaders, not "soloists." It is about planting seeds that lead to a mutual creation or collaboration. We live in a culture and a time that promotes soloists—and it's not just about ego-driven leaders seeking the solo spotlight. The challenge is that sometimes members of our congregations and communities like the idea of a "soloist" being responsible for making change, because a soloist lets them off the hook. A song leader, on the other hand, requires them to join in, to do their part—the hard, daily work of advocating for children. I wonder how each of us might work against that soloist culture to become song leaders building the children's movement, organizing in our own spheres and in our own communities.

What is the seed that you are called to plant, as a song leader, that will engage others in your neighborhood or networks, congregation or community, in creating a new song of justice for children, a new voice, a new level of action? How do we create an explosion of justice in our day?

I Had Never Been That Me Before

This new song isn't just about the kind of leadership and collaboration that the movement needs. It is also about transforming our understanding of ourselves, our calling, our power that will not be silenced. Bernice Johnson Reagon, looking back, observes, "The voice I have now I got the first time I sang in a movement meeting, after I got out of jail. I did the song, 'Over My Head I See Freedom in the Air,' but I had never heard that voice before. I had never been that *me* before. And once I became that me, I have never let that me go . . . a transformation took place inside of the people. The singing was just the echo of that."

Bernice continues, "They could not stop our sound. They would have to kill us to stop us from singing. Sometimes the police would plead and say, 'Please stop singing.' And you would just know that your word was being heard, and you felt joy. There is a way in which those songs kept us from being touched by people who would want us not to be who we were becoming."[9]

"Sing to God a new song! Play your best with *joyful* shouts! God loves righteousness and justice; God's faithful love fills the whole earth."

I wonder, what is the transformation that God will bring about in each of us; what new voice will we discover as we take new action? Surely part of our job is lifting a new song that will surround our children with such love and power and justice that they cannot "be touched by people who do not want them to be who they are becoming."

Mandela and Francois, Barbara, and Bernice, all found new voices, new songs, new ways in the midst of bleak times to exceed even their own expectations of themselves, to lead others into the movement, and to proclaim God's justice with new voices that refused to be silenced. Can we do any less? *Sing to God a new song! Play your best with joyful shouts! Because God's word is right, God's every act is done in good faith. God loves righteousness and justice; God's faithful love fills the whole earth."* May it be so. Amen.

~

Questions for Faithful Response

1. Have you felt that our children's or grandchildren's future is bleak? What do you see that makes you feel that way?
2. We need a new song. Not a song set to music per se but a new song—metaphorically—that will unite, inspire, and

encourage us to exceed our expectations to build a nation fit for children even when, especially when, the future looks bleak. What is the "new song" that you would like to "sing" through your work, witness, organizing, advocacy, preaching, or protests that will declare and help to usher in God's righteousness, justice, and love? If your new song of action had a title, what would it be?

3. The new song that we are called to sing through our words, work, and witness is one that engages the community in its creation. Who could you envision partnering with to make a difference for children? How might you reach out to engage them?

4. Bernice Johnson Reagon said, "I had never been that *me* before." Singing a new song of faithful action is also about transforming our understanding of ourselves, our calling, and our power that will not be silenced. Have you ever had a transformative experience when you discovered a "new me" that you had never been before? What is the further transformation that you hope God will bring about in you? What new voice do you hope to discover as you take new action?

5. Part of our calling is lifting a new song that will surround our children with such love and power and justice that they cannot, in Bernice Johnson Reagon's words, "be touched by people who do not want them to be who they are becoming." What are ways that you surround children to protect them from negative, limiting, or constraining people or influences? How is this task most demanding for parents and others raising or caring for children of color? For children in poverty? For children who are in the LGBTQ community? How do you cultivate in children a sense of their own power?

6. *Especially for parents and caregivers:* Teach your child the simple hymn "I'm Gonna Live So God Can Use Me," whose lyrics are "I'm gonna live so God can use me, anywhere, Lord, any time" repeated three times. The verses

then substitute "live" with other words such as "work" and "pray." Discuss with your children how God can use their and your lives, work, and prayers to help others, including other children. Your children may come up with new verses too: substituting words like "play," "learn," and "speak."

Chapter Three

Stumbling Blocks and Cornerstones

Isaiah 28

In that day the LORD of hosts will be a garland of glory,
 and a diadem of beauty, to the remnant of [God's] people;
and a spirit of justice to the one who sits in judgment,
 and strength to those who turn back the battle at the gate.

These also reel with wine
 and stagger with strong drink;
the priest and the prophet reel with strong drink,
 they are confused with wine,
 they stagger with strong drink;
they err in vision,
 they stumble in giving judgment.
All tables are covered with filthy vomit;
 no place is clean.
. . . .
Therefore hear the word of the LORD, you scoffers
 who rule this people in Jerusalem.
Because you have said, "We have made a covenant with death,
 and with Sheol we have an agreement;
when the overwhelming scourge passes through
 it will not come to us;

for we have made lies our refuge,
  and in falsehood we have taken shelter";
therefore thus says the Lord God,
See, I am laying in Zion a foundation stone,
  a tested stone,
a precious cornerstone, a sure foundation:
  "One who trusts will not panic."
And I will make justice the line, and righteousness the
  plummet;
hail will sweep away the refuge of lies,
  and waters will overwhelm the shelter.

(Isa. 28:5–8, 14–17)

The Freshman Step and Stumbling Blocks

My older sister and younger brother and I all happened to attend the same university—each entering several years apart. My sister had been at the school two years already and was showing me, the newbie, around the campus. We went to the post office, a flight of stairs below street level, and then instead of exiting the way we had entered, she said, "Let's go out this door at the back."

We started walking up the stone steps, with me following her, when I stumbled. She looked back with that wicked gleam that perhaps big sisters never lose and said, "That's the freshman step."

Huh?

In that flight of stairs leading from the post office up to street level, one stone step was just slightly higher than the others that preceded it and followed it. It was called the freshman step because first-year students always stumbled on it.

Hundreds of years before, when the steps were being built, I imagine the stone mason was just a little sloppy, rather than malicious, in failing to measure well enough. Nonetheless, for centuries it has been a stumbling block to the innocent newcomer—unless those older and more experienced take time to warn them, to show them how to step carefully so as not to stumble.

Now, I mentioned that I had a younger brother who followed me to the same university. I'd like to say that my own experience of stumbling—the surprise, embarrassment, even hurt—created in me a determination to protect him, warn him of the difficulty, and help him over it. I'm ashamed—yes, decades later, still ashamed—to say that when my younger brother first came to campus, I, with that same wicked, big-sister gleam, took him to stumble on the freshman step himself. I knew better, but I still did it.

The real stumbling block there wasn't the step itself but the casual cruelty I exhibited—using the position of being more experienced, more powerful, in-the-know, to take advantage rather than help. The real stumbling block was the failure to act differently, to have the expectation be not that you introduce new students by watching them stumble but that you welcome them by helping them step over the obstacle and safely make their way to higher ground.

Stumbling Blocks from Isaiah's Day to Our Own

That block my brother stumbled on was, of course, relatively benign, its negative impact short-lived. But since the earliest days, those who should protect and guide, those who should lead from experience with compassion and justice, have instead been letting—often, in fact, causing—those who count on them to stumble.

In Isaiah's day, the prophet, on God's behalf, took to task those who were causing or letting others stumble. In Isaiah 28, the prophet was speaking difficult words to those who had strayed from God's intended justice, righteousness, and compassion. He spoke words of woe to the people, words of warning to the priests and the prophets, words of judgment over the political leadership. People, priests, prophets, politicians—all were missing the mark. "They err in vision, they stumble in giving judgment" (v. 7b), and, later, they have "made lies [their] refuge, and in falsehood [they] have taken shelter" (v. 15b).

Hundreds of years later, Jesus would offer his own strong words of condemnation of those who place stumbling blocks in the way of children. "It would be better for you if a great millstone were fastened around your neck and you were drowned in the depth of the sea," he said (Matt. 18:6b).

Today can we hear words of woe, warning, and judgment—whether we are in pew or pulpit, whether political leaders or members of the public? Have we erred in vision, stumbled in judgment? What would Isaiah say about our collective failure if he knew that in our rich nation:

- Every 2 seconds during the school year a public school student receives an out-of-school suspension.
- Every 9 seconds during the school year a public high school student drops out.
- Every 24 seconds a child is arrested.
- Every 34 seconds a baby is born into poverty.
- Every 45 seconds a child is abused or neglected.
- Every 67 seconds a baby is born into extreme poverty.
- Every 3 hours and 28 minutes a child or teen is killed by a gun.
- Every 6 hours a child is killed by abuse or neglect.[1]

These are stumbling blocks that all who are in positions to make a difference should be removing rather than accepting, giving up on, or despairing of. They are stumbling blocks we should be guiding children over or around or removing altogether. (Sometimes statistics themselves can be stumbling blocks; they can add to our numbness so that we forget the living, breathing, hurting, hoping children behind each one, the names behind the numbers and the stories behind the statistics.)

From Stumbling Blocks to Foundation Stone

The stumbling blocks strewn in front of children and poor families are real, but the good news is they are not the end of the story—not the end of the story for children, for the church, or for our nation and world. Despite the stumbling blocks for which the people, priests, prophets, and political leaders together bore responsibility and the stumbling blocks for which citizens, congregation members, clergy, child advocates, and elected representatives bear responsibility—even in the midst of words of

warning and woe and judgment—came these words of promise
and possibility from Isaiah:

> Therefore thus says the Lord GOD,
> See, I am laying in Zion a foundation stone,
>   a tested stone,
> a precious cornerstone, a sure foundation:
>   [inscribed] "One who trusts will not panic."
> And I will make justice the measuring line,
>   and righteousness the plummet.
>   (Isa. 28:16–17a)

Instead of the stumbling blocks of injustice, God gives us a
cornerstone, a sure foundation for which *justice* is the measuring
line, *righteousness* the plumb line. Scholar Gene Tucker writes of
this passage:

> In Isaiah, the stone concerns not the Messiah, or the Davidic
> King, but Zion as God's chosen and secure place. . . . The
> inscribed stone is a symbol of assurance, of the good news of
> God's presence. But at the same time the good news is a test.
> The leaders and the people are called to respond in faith to
> this good news. This faith, however, is not the affirmation
> of particular beliefs, but trust in God and living according to
> justice and righteousness.[2]

According to Tucker, "Justice and righteousness will be the measure of faith and action."[3]

In ancient times, a plummet—also known as a plumb line—was
a simple tool used to show a true vertical line, made of nothing
more than a string with a weight at one end. When it was important to build something well, with truly vertical walls and accurate
measurements, builders would use a measuring line and plummet.
If they didn't, the structure would not be strong and might col-
lapse. We who claim Christ as our cornerstone, our sure foundation, must build a church, communities, nation, and world in
which *justice* is the measuring line and righteousness the plummet.

What does it look like when justice is the measuring line? Those who need justice the most can teach those of us who would be their advocates. Gary Bellow learned that. Gary Bellow was a Harvard Law School professor, the founder and former faculty director of the school's clinical programs, and a pioneering public interest lawyer who worked with Caesar Chavez and the United Farm Workers. He also worked with the Children's Defense Fund, contributing to CDF's earliest work on children in adult jails. Four years before he died, at the age of just sixty-four, he shared this experience in a speech at the 1996 Alliance for Justice annual luncheon:

> Thirty years ago, or maybe more now, I represented a man in Bakersfield, California. His name was Juan Rivera. I represented him in an action to get back a repossessed truck that he owned and had been taken from him.
>
> For those of you who can imagine what it is like to work from the Mexican border to Washington [state], picking crops from April to October, you'll understand that this truck was his lifeline, the only way to earn his living. And he had lost his truck. Actually, he had beaten the hell out of the guy who tried to repossess it. I was appointed to represent him to get him out of jail, and in the process of getting the case dismissed he asked me if I could try to get his truck back.
>
> So there I was, armed with a lot of new legal contract theories and some California consumer protection law, filing suit for the return of the truck in the Superior Court of Marin County. We went to trial or preliminary hearing in about three weeks.
>
> During the recess at that hearing, Juan came out and sat next to me on a bench. And he looked at me and said, "We're going to lose, aren't we?"
>
> And I think I probably said something really stupid like, "There's always hope" or "you ain't seen nothing yet."
>
> Because he was much older and much smarter than I was, he looked at me and said, "I think I should tell the judge that I need that truck more than the company [that was repossessing it]."

Now I almost said back to him what every lawyer . . . knows: that the judge doesn't give a damn about whether you need the truck more than the company. That's not a viable legal theory. But for some reason I didn't. Instead I looked at him and said, "Why not?"

And we went back into that courtroom, and Juan took the stand. And he told the judge about how he lived and how he earned his living and how he fed his children and how he cared for and constantly repaired that truck and how he couldn't pay for it [not this year nor maybe even next year] but he needed it.

It was a remarkable performance. As I stood there, and as the lawyer for the opposition, I think his name was Mr. Brown, stood up to cross-examine, the judge looked at him and said, "Mr. Brown, I think you should give Mr. Rivera back his truck and take a tax deduction on it."

Brown stiffened and said, "I can't do that, your honor."

And the judge said, "You can't take the tax deduction, Mr. Brown, or you can't give him back his truck?"

And then Brown looked at the judge and said, "Oh hell, why not."

And Juan Rivera walked out of that courtroom with an order giving him the right to repossess back the repossessed truck that was in a yard some distance from the courthouse. Reflecting on the experience, Gary said: "Now I don't want to get too romantic about his story. I never saw that judge do a kind or thoughtful thing again in three years. I don't believe Mr. Brown ever gave anyone else back his truck. And we sued his company twice in consumer fraud cases, and he never mentioned that afternoon. And those of you who know me well know that I did not come to the conclusion that people are inherently good or the system really works or that all you really need is the right argument to win a case.

But I did see an act of justice that day. An occasion when power responded to persuasion in the right way at the right time. And I've had a life where I've been lucky enough to have more than my share of those moments. And it has given me passion, and it has given me purpose throughout a career. What

I didn't understand then and what I want to close with now is that the perseverance and discipline that is so much a part of the work the public interest community does depends on those occasions of justice. And on the belief that more will come. In a time when you can talk about racial justice and be told you're engaged in social interest pleading or you can be worried about 14.5 million poor children and be told that's soft-headed liberalism, *we have to nurture the belief in that possibility that occasions of justice can occur in large numbers in many places. We have to work like hell to create those occasions.* We have to think hard about those times, as Juan Rivera taught me, when conscience and commitment shape a better strategy and make a better argument than the shallow pragmatism that we bring to our work. We have to ask again and again whether or not each small act we're engaged in, each small fight we engage in is an important one, regardless of whether or not it gets celebrity or whether or not it is large in scale. Bobby Kennedy said this much better than I did; here is what he said: "It is from numerous diverse acts of courage and belief that human history is shaped. Each time a person stands up for an ideal or acts to improve the lot of others or strikes out against injustice, he or she sends a tiny ripple of hope and crossing each other from a million different centers of energy and daring, these ripples can send down a current which can sweep down the mightiest walls of oppression and resistance."

Now I remember again very vividly as I walked down the stairs of the Bakersfield courthouse, around the corner came Juan Rivera and his truck. I had been there over an hour and he had managed to get his truck back. I jumped up on the running board. . . . And I shook his hand because in the truck were his wife and his kids.

And he said to me, "Do you need a lift?" and I said, "No, I have a way home."

And then he said, and smiled in that wonderful smile that was a gift that people can sometimes give each other, "I have a way home too, amigo. Thank you for believing in me."

Now the fact is that it was <u>his</u> belief, *not mine, that you could wrench a better future out of an unjust present that made a difference.* It is well to remember that it has always been that way and with enough effort it always will."[4]

While we work for justice to roll down like water, let us be grateful for each tiny ripple. While we work to change the odds for all children, let us be sustained by the hope of each child who beats the odds. While we yearn for a whole loaf to sustain us as we hunger for the promised land, may we be sustained by the merest manna, a taste of the bread of life. Let us affirm with Gary Bellow that, by God's grace, we can "wrench a better future out of an unjust present" and that we will make a difference for our children. We must hold fast to the plumb line of justice and commit to replacing stumbling blocks with the cornerstone of a justice for all our children. May it be so. Amen.

∿

Questions for Faithful Response

1. What are the stumbling blocks before children and families that concern you most?

2. How did you feel when you read the statistics about the state of America's children? What do you think it will take to change those statistics? What can you do?

3. The prophet saw responsibility for injustice spread across the people, the political leaders, and the religious community. What role or responsibility do you see each bearing in the problems our children face today? What role or responsibility do you see for each to solve them?

4. Gary Bellow said, "I did see an act of justice that day—an occasion when power responded to persuasion in the right way at the right time." When have you seen an act of justice as Gary defined it?

5. Gary Bellow acknowledges that idealism about change is derided. He challenges us to consider times when a

committed idealism shapes a better strategy than shallow pragmatism. Do you feel pulled toward idealism or pragmatism? What are the advantages and disadvantages of each?

6. *For parents and other caregivers:* Stumbling blocks and plumb lines can work as visual metaphors for children who are elementary-aged and older. Gather rocks with your children, and then name the stumbling blocks they see facing other children or themselves, and talk about how to remove them. Or make your own plumb lines with string and a weight (like a round metal washer from the hardware store) as you talk about how plumb lines were used to build things strong and straight and true. Hang it somewhere to remember your family's commitment to work for justice.

Chapter Four

Troops, Trumpets, and Torches

Judges 7

After [Gideon] divided the three hundred men into three companies, and put trumpets into the hands of all of them, and empty jars, with torches inside the jars, he said to them, "Look at me, and do the same; when I come to the outskirts of the camp, do as I do. When I blow the trumpet, I and all who are with me, then you also blow the trumpets around the whole camp, and shout, 'For the Lord and for Gideon!'"

So Gideon and the hundred who were with him came to the outskirts of the camp at the beginning of the middle watch, when they had just set the watch; and they blew the trumpets and smashed the jars that were in their hands. So the three companies blew the trumpets and broke the jars, holding in their left hands the torches, and in their right hands the trumpets to blow; and they cried, "A sword for the Lord and for Gideon!" Every man stood in his place all around the camp, and all the men in camp ran; they cried out and fled. When they blew the three hundred trumpets, the Lord set every man's sword against his fellow and against all the army; and the army fled as far as Beth-shittah toward Zererah, as far as the border of Abel-meholah, by Tabbath.

(Judg. 7:16–22)

The Biblical Story

It was late at night; silence and shadow shrouded the valley of Jezreel where the oppressors were encamped. They slept snug and smug in the valley—they had pushed around the Israelites so long that they figured they'd beaten them down for good. Hadn't they forced them from homes and into hiding in caves—rendering them homeless? Hadn't they destroyed their crops and animals, their livelihood—leaving them jobless? Hadn't they poured into the Israelites' communities, devastated them, and then departed—leaving them "greatly impoverished"? Homeless, jobless, greatly impoverished, the Israelites cried out to God.

God's response to the injustice, to the cry of the Israelites, was to commission Gideon to rally the troops to defeat the injustice and rout the oppressive regime. Gideon wasn't the most likely candidate for the job. God called him mighty when he seemed weak and anxious. Gideon tried to hide, and God found him. Gideon was called, and he argued with the angel. God showed him patience when Gideon dragged his feet rather than moving swiftly toward his call. He had launched his first test campaign at night, in secret, pulling down the symbol of idolatry in his own community to restore their focus on the God of love and justice.

Gideon finally started to trust God. He was ready to follow God's leading to take on the mighty oppression. And so Gideon put out the call for supporters, sounding the trumpet himself and sending others, messengers, who could spread out on the ground and summon the other tribes to join the movement, the battle. Many responded in a first flurry of enthusiasm.

But then God insisted that it wasn't quantity but character and commitment that were needed: fewer were needed in the struggle so that the focus would be on God's triumph and not their own accomplishment. So those who were fearful—two-thirds of them—were sent back home. So now Gideon had those around him who were prepared for courageous action.

But just being courageous wasn't enough. God needed people who were ready to act with urgency. The remaining people were sent to drink from a river. Some flung themselves down to lap like dogs, wasting no time, focused on speed. Others knelt carefully, daintily scooping water to their mouths. And what about those who had worried more about decorum than urgency? They were sent home too—this was no time to worry about appearance; a sense of urgency was what was needed.

Most important, God insisted that Gideon and his troops recognize that they didn't need big numbers, just big hearts, big courage, and big trust that God's own hand would be responsible for the victory to come.

So here Gideon was—finally trusting God's plan and ready to initiate a wise strategy. He had put out the call and rallied the troops, and though he didn't have huge numbers, he knew he could count on the committed, courageous few by his side who would act with urgency. Most important, they were strengthened by the conviction that they could count on God to win the victory, knowing that the victory would be God's and not theirs.

Those who were left, determined and confident, were prepared to resist even if the methods sounded outlandish. Their actions would underscore that the victory belonged to God, not to their military might. Not one of them held a sword in hand; instead, each held in one hand a trumpet—that is, a ram's horn, a shofar—and in the other a torch, hidden for now inside a clay jar.

Gideon's side knew what they were up against. They knew the opposition had the big numbers on its side. But Gideon's force also knew the opposition's weakness. Even now, some in the opposition were anxious; word was spreading from one to another that a dream had revealed they were not to remain in power for long. Gideon's forces could take advantage of that uneasiness. Also, they were literally and figuratively on higher ground, which would also help them win.

They surrounded the opposition—they weren't going to take on just a part but saw the big picture, the comprehensive whole that had to be defeated. They also had a vision of what they would put in place once they defeated the oppressors. This vision was nothing short of a complete restoration of their community, a return to life where there were homes and a livelihood for all, where no one suffered from poverty.

Gideon, that unlikely leader who had started as the youngest child of the weakest tribe, had emerged from the midst of the people as the leader. He remained in the fray, saying, "Do as I do. Listen for the sound of the trumpet." Gideon knew that the victory would be God's but that it also took human agency to win, and so the call was "for God and for Gideon." (The danger and eventual downfall of overreaching in his sense of self-importance is another meditation for another day.)

The trumpets rang out. The mighty cry went up in unison. The bright light revealed the oppressors. And every one of Gideon's people stood their ground. They didn't run away. They didn't run in to attack. They stood their ground.

The show of unity, determination, and coordination, along with a higher calling that played on the growing fears and weakness of the powerful, put the oppressors on the run. The opponents were in chaos compared to the coordination of Gideon's troops: they ran while Gideon's people stood their ground; they turned their weapons on one another while Gideon's troops held their torches and trumpets in hand. Gideon's troops routed the opposition.

Thousands of years later, Gene Sharp, noted strategist for nonviolent revolutions against oppressive regimes, wrote, "Against a strong self-reliant force, given wise strategy, disciplined and courageous action, and genuine strength, the dictatorship will eventually crumble."[1] But in the biblical account, all that Gideon and those at his side knew was that the oppressive powers had taken flight.

The Historical Story

Millennia later, silence and shadow shrouded the city streets in America as a father led his child, little Florence Kelley, on a tour of glass and steel factories at midnight. They opened the factory door and were surrounded by light and noise as they witnessed other children toiling long into the night, exhaustion, hunger, and resignation stooping the children's small shoulders as they bent over the dangerous, whirring machines or processed molten glass in fiery furnaces.

The oppressive forces maintaining child labor in the late nineteenth and early twentieth centuries were impressive, entrenched and encamped: big business profited from it; legislators lagged; the courts caved and overturned the measures that would have made a difference; the media muted itself; and the public looked away. All the while, two million little children toiled long hours, earning pitiful wages instead of an education as they suffered, were maimed, and even died.

In the wake of these seemingly insurmountable forces, a small but mighty band came together to rout this injustice. There was a circle of trumpet blowers and torchbearers who rallied for the fight, working fearlessly and urgently to end the oppression. Let me tell you about just two.

Florence Kelley never forgot the injustice her progressive father had taken her to see that night in an early version of a "Child Watch,"[2] and as an adult she became a trumpet first in the battle to end child labor and then as a board member of the nascent NAACP. In 1891 she went to Chicago and lived at Hull House—the pioneering settlement house that provided child care, classes, employment and other services, and advocacy to improve the lives of immigrants and others in poverty. Her first fieldwork was an intensive survey of the square mile surrounding the settlement—a precursor to CDF's door-knocking research for the report *Children Out of School*. As she went door to door, Florence Kelley found children as young as three working in tenements manufacturing garments. As a result of her research and other studies, the Illinois state legislature passed the first factory law prohibiting employment of children under age fourteen. She pioneered the use of labels on clothing to certify that garments had been produced without child labor. She sounded the trumpet with moral heat and cold, hard facts. In December 1920 congressional testimony, she compared Congress's indifference to the daily deaths of 680 American children to Herod's slaughter of the innocents. She was a trumpet and a torch as she sounded the call and shone light on the injustice of child labor.

Florence Kelley wasn't the only one to rally the troops and become a trumpet blower and torchbearer in the battle against child labor. Mother Jones held her trumpet and torch high as well, rallying the troops and helping to win the battle. A former dressmaker, Mary Harris "Mother" Jones became an enormously influential speaker and community organizer on behalf of workers' rights and other justice concerns. During a trip to Kensington, Pennsylvania, Mother Jones was outraged at the flagrant continuation of child labor despite earlier state laws on the books. Sixteen thousand children were working there, in paper mills and other factories, most just nine or ten years old.

She asked newspaper reporters why they weren't publishing the facts about child labor in Pennsylvania. She recounted later their answer: "They said they couldn't because the mill owners had stock in the papers. 'Well,' she said, 'I've got stock in these little children, and I'll arrange a little publicity.'"[3]

They assembled children one morning in Philadelphia's Independence Park and from there paraded with banners to the courthouse to hold a meeting publicizing the cruelty of child labor. A massive crowd gathered in the public square in front of the city hall—with the officials of city hall standing in the open windows. As the people saw firsthand the injured children, Mother Jones decried that "their little lives went out to make wealth for others, that neither state or city officials paid any attention to these wrongs, and that they did not care that these children were to be the future citizens of the nation."

She wrote, "I called upon the millionaire manufacturers to cease their moral murders, and I cried to the officials in the open windows opposite, 'Someday the workers will take possession of your city hall, and when we do, no child will be sacrificed on the altar of profit.'" She was a trumpet! She recalled, "The officials quickly closed the windows, as they had closed their eyes and hearts." However, the newspapers picked up the story, and "the universities discussed it. Preachers began talking. That was what I wanted," she said. "Public attention on the subject of child labor."

After a time, attention drifted from the tragedy of child labor, and Mother Jones determined that "the people needed stirring up again." She thought about the crowds that were turning out to see the Liberty Bell, which was being toured around the country.

Reflecting that the children were striking for the freedom childhood should have, she decided that they too should go on tour,
starting with a mass meeting in Philadelphia and marching on to
see President Roosevelt vacationing in New York to urge him to
have Congress enact legislation "prohibiting the exploitation of
childhood." She observed, wryly, "I thought that President Roosevelt might see these mill children and compare them with his
own little ones who were spending the summer on the seashore
at Oyster Bay. I thought too, out of politeness, we might call
on Morgan in Wall Street who owned the mines where many of
these children's fathers worked."

She called them an "army." With the permission of the parents
and the help of a few adults, they set off—each with a knapsack
carrying a plate and cup, walking about ten miles each day. One
child played a fife, another, a drum—that was their "band." They
carried banners that said, "We want more schools and less hos-
pitals." "We want time to play." "Prosperity is here. Where is
ours?" The children were trumpets in the battle, too, and torches
who shed a light on all that they were suffering themselves. As
they travelled, they held meetings where the children themselves
showed the horrors of child labor. When in one town the mayor
insisted that Mother Jones and the children could not hold a
rally because he lacked police protection for them, Mother Jones
pointed out, "These little children have never known any sort of
protection, your honor . . . and they are used to going without it.
He let us have our meeting," she said.

When they reached New Jersey, Mother Jones asked the
mayor of Princeton for permission to speak "about higher education" across the street from the Princeton University campus.
A crowd including professors, students, and townspeople gathered, and she schooled them, denouncing the rich for "robb[ing]
these little children of any education of the lowest order that they
might send their sons and daughters to places of higher education. . . . Here's a text book on economics," she said, pointing
to 10-year-old James Ashworth, already stooped from his work
bearing heavy loads. "He gets three dollars a week and his sister
who is fourteen gets six dollars," said Mother Jones. "They work

in a carpet factory ten hours a day while the children of the rich are getting their higher education."

Mother Jones recalled that later that night, "We camped on the banks of Stony Brook where years and years before the ragged Revolutionary Army camped, Washington's brave soldiers that made their fight for freedom." They reached New York and her trumpet continued:

> In Georgia where children work day and night in the cotton mills they have just passed a bill to protect song birds. What about little children from whom all song is gone? . . . I will tell the president that the prosperity he boasts of is prosperity of the rich wrung from the poor and the helpless. . . . The trouble is that no one in Washington cares. I saw our legislators in one hour pass three bills for the relief of the railways but when labor cries for aid for the children they will not listen. I asked a man in prison once how he happened to be there and he said he had stolen a pair of shoes. I told him if he had stolen a railroad he would be a United States Senator.

Finally the children reached Oyster Bay, but President Roosevelt refused to see them or to respond to Mother Jones's letters. Nonetheless, the march had been a success, focusing the nation's attention on the crime of child labor. Although the children were forced back to work, soon after a child labor law was passed by the Pennsylvania legislature that freed thousands of children from mill work and kept many more from entering the factories at all.

These women trumpets and torches were joined by others who helped surround the forces of injustice, including Louis Brandeis, who worked the legal system, and Lewis Hine, a school teacher who left teaching to photograph the injustice of child labor. Hine sneaked into factories under various pretexts, taking photographs of the children and surreptitiously interviewing them, scribbling notes with his hand hidden in his pocket. It was a battle that stretched over decades but was finally won.

Our Story

One hundred and some years later, it is late at night, and silence and shadow shroud our nation—where injustice slumbers, unaware that it is soon to be routed. But maybe there is already a whisper, a word that God is on the side of justice and that the oppression of children and those who are poor won't last forever.

Now is the time for our "grand strategy," in the words of Gene Sharp. We stand on higher ground and know that God is on the side of justice. Now is the time to encompass the whole force of oppression and the injustices facing our children with a strategy that uses the few but the fearless, those who don't care about appearance but have a sense of urgency, who trust enough to try the unconventional. Each of us is called to help rally the troops and take up a trumpet and torch.

Who are the troops that you will rally? Like Gideon, we will need to summon some of the troops ourselves, and others will come because we have sent out messengers on the ground who can spread out and reach various tribes to come together for the battle. Like Gideon, we may find that all who come are not prepared for the struggle—those who are not committed and those who are not courageous don't need to stick around. What we need are those who are committed and courageous and who have a sense of urgency—those who don't worry about decorum and appearance but who will do what it takes as fast as they can to join the struggle. With God's help, we can win with a small but mighty army.

How will we organize? Who will we organize, and how will we find the kind of strategy that uses the few to rout the mighty? Who are the troops that you will rally—children and parents, young people, people of faith, lawyers, people who have been incarcerated? Who will share our sense of courage, urgency, and commitment to the strategy? How will you organize them to join the struggle? How do we keep ourselves and those who rally with us centered on God's leading, God's justice, and God's capacity to triumph?

How will you be a trumpet? Gideon blew a trumpet to start rallying the troops, but others had to help. Gideon blew the trumpet to signal the start of the struggle, but it only worked because all the people there held their own trumpets in hand and blew their trumpets when it was time. With just one trumpet or a few they would have been defeated. Only the sound of all the trumpets blown in unison could create the kind of mighty sound that terrified the opposition and put them on the run.

They blew their trumpets in unison, but the sound was not uniform. The trumpets were shofars, ram's horns. Brass horns all sound the same; with shofars, each one has a different sound. What is the unique sound of the trumpet that you are called to blow? How will you be a trumpet? What truth, what story, what testimony will you tell to build the movement for children? What is the noise you will make, the word you will proclaim?

How will we amplify the message that justice must triumph over injustice? How do we make our sound heard over the din of distraction in our world today, over the noise of nonsense, over the competing claims on time and attention? What kind of mighty clamor can we make to draw attention to children's needs and strike fear in the hearts of those who harm our children?

How will you be a torch? One torch alone wouldn't have illuminated the opposition, wouldn't have shown the opposition that they were surrounded—just one torch or a few would have shown the opposition just whom to attack. Again, they would have been defeated if it had just been Gideon and one or two others. *Every* torch was needed—they needed to have the opposition surrounded.

They didn't have big boxes of Diamond matches back then. I think about how the torches were lit—one person lighting a torch and then leaning over to light the next person's, and so on. We are called to be torchbearers and also torch sharers.

How will you be a torchbearer in the coming days and years? What truth, what injustice will you shed light on? How will you help people see child suffering? What is the torch you are called to carry that will illuminate the oppression, throw the unjust into a panic, and rout them from power? How will you shed light so that we see our way forward? How will you share your torch with others? For God calls us to stand our ground in such a way that those who work against our children take flight.

Every one of us has troops to rally, trumpets to blow, and torches to hold high, to bear, and to share if we are going to rout the oppression once and for all. When we are organized, truly organized, when each of us has a trumpet in one hand and a torch in the other, and when we act in concert so that our sound and light are amplified, we will by the grace of God rout the entrenched forces of injustice, throw them into disarray, and put them on the run once and for all. Thanks be to God.

∼

Questions for Faithful Response

1. God often chooses the least likely for challenging and prophetic tasks. When or in what ways have you felt inadequate to the charge God has given you?

2. Who are the troops that you will rally to improve the lives of children and work against injustice? Who will you connect with that shares your sense of courage, urgency, and commitment to the strategy?

3. How do we keep ourselves and those who rally with us centered on God's leading, God's justice, and God's capacity to triumph?

4. How will you be a trumpet? What truth, what story, what testimony will you tell to build the movement for children? How can we amplify the message that justice must triumph over injustice? How do we make our sound heard over the din of distraction and competing claims in our world today?

5. How will you be torchbearer and a torch sharer in the coming days and years? What particular injustice are you called to shed light on? What is the unique torch you can carry to illuminate oppression and rout the unjust from power?

6. ***Especially for parents and other caregivers:*** Retell the story of Gideon in age-appropriate ways with your children (younger children might enjoy acting it out or providing sound effects). Discuss how Gideon wasn't the oldest or biggest but learned to trust God and became a strong leader, using good thinking and loyal partners to scare off their opponents. Is there a problem facing them or other children? What good thinking and loyal partners—children or adults—could help them solve it?

Part II

Challenged

Chapter Five

What's Next?

Jonah

Now the word of the LORD came to Jonah son of Amittai, saying, "Go at once to Nineveh, that great city, and cry out against it; for their wickedness has come up before me." But Jonah set out to flee to Tarshish from the presence of the LORD. He went down to Joppa and found a ship going to Tarshish; so he paid his fare and went on board, to go with them to Tarshish, away from the presence of the LORD.

(Jonah 1:1–3)

Until recently, when I've heard the story of Jonah, I've always kind of assumed he was sitting on his hands watching soaps or SportsCenter until God came to him with the call to go to Nineveh. I just figured he was a slacker, a shirker. It hadn't really occurred to me that we don't know what Jonah was doing before that first verse.

For most prophets, Scripture tells us about that moment when they first embarked on their prophetic career and what they were doing until that moment: For Amos, the text tells us about his shift from shepherd to prophet. We read about Jeremiah's being called and demurring that he is just a boy. Ezekiel, the text tells us, was a priest when he was called to more prophetic

49

proclamation. We know what they were doing before they were first called.

In Jonah's case, maybe the absence of this information is because Jonah's call to prophetic activity had happened years before and he had already been hard at it. In this first verse of the book of Jonah, perhaps we're just coming to his prophetic life midstream. Perhaps here God is not calling him to prophetic activity for the first time—this may just be his latest assignment, the newest chapter in his prophetic mission.

Maybe he was already knee-deep in prophetic work. Maybe he was already staying at the office until 11 at night, or all but living on an airplane, or networking with the temples in his hometown. (You'll recall that later in the story, Jonah is fast asleep on the ship while others are up panicking; that sounds to me like someone who has been burning the candle at both ends and is desperate for rest, not for a new assignment like Nineveh.)

Maybe he was already doing all that he thought he could or should—content with his existing call, feeling good about what he was doing and where he was doing it.

And here comes God with the next call, the next mission: get up and go to Nineveh.

Nineveh? *No, anywhere but Nineveh! Not there; not them.* There was something different in Jonah's mind about this call to Nineveh. There was something about Nineveh that made him want to run in the other direction.

Huge, Hostile, Hopeless, and Hard

So what was it about Nineveh? For starters, it was huge. In our Scripture passage, God called it "great." It was "great" in various senses of the word. It was great in size—it took three days to walk across. It was great in population—some 120,000 inhabitants. It was great in political influence. It was the capitol city of Assyria—where the leadership made decisions that affected the nation itself as well as the weaker nations that they controlled. Nineveh was the capitol of the enemy—the nation that had ruthlessly conquered Israel in 722 and expelled its inhabitants and all but obliterated Judah in 701. And despite its having gotten so badly off track, it was greatly important to God. Ironically, all the things that made Nineveh "great" contributed to Jonah's reluctance to go there—it was just too huge a task.

Nineveh wasn't just huge, however. It was, Jonah presumed, hostile—hostile to him and his message. Nineveh's people weren't Jonah's people. These were the utterly detested "other"—the enemy who had wrought destruction on Jonah's people. They were from a different region, ethnicity, and religion. They had different values, different politics—politics that seemed focused on doing harm to Jonah's people. They weren't his kind, and he assumed they would be hostile to him and to the message he brought from his God.

Nineveh was not only huge and hostile; it was also hopeless. Nineveh is described elsewhere in Scripture as a "city of bloodshed, utterly deceitful, full of booty [with] no end to the plunder" (Nah. 3:1) and as a supremely arrogant city that "lived secure, that said to itself, 'I am, and there is no one else'" (Zeph. 2:15). God talked point blank about Nineveh's "wickedness." That much injustice must have seemed to Jonah simply hopeless to change.

It was huge, hostile, and hopeless; it was just plain hard. Why, oh why did this have to be what God called him to next? Why not an easy assignment—why not prophetic work among his own people? Why not pastoral work, a smaller place, a more amenable community? On top of everything, what if he wound up looking like a fool—either because he couldn't get the job done or because he was so effective, created such change, that it looked like things weren't as bad as he said? No way; Jonah was having none of it, and he let his feet do the talking.

Our Own Ninevehs

I think that all of us, at various times, have a Nineveh—the call that we'd rather not hear and, if we hear it, the call that we'd rather not heed. It's not that we're shirkers or slackers or just sitting around; it's just that we get that sinking feeling of, "O Lord, no, not Nineveh. Anything but Nineveh. It's just too huge, or

hostile, or hopeless, or hard." Even the most dedicated prophets have their Ninevehs—the places, communities, or issues that
give them pause, that make them turn away before they turn to
face them.

Vincent Harding, friend and colleague of Dr. Martin Luther
King Jr., wrote in his book *Martin Luther King: The Inconvenient
Hero*, "The sense of revolutionary vocation did not come easily
to King. It was not the life for which he once had thought he was
preparing. The relatively secure joint career of pastor and college
professor had seemed an attractive possibility while he worked on
his doctoral studies."[1] I suspect that for Dr. King, Nineveh may
have looked a little like Montgomery . . . or Selma or Cicero or
taking on the issue of Vietnam.

Dr. Harding continues, describing King's decision to speak
out about Vietnam:

> But by 1967 [King] saw no escape from God's movement
> in history, and its urgent summons to a life of creative inse-
> curity. So, with much fear and trembling, he answered the
> call, saying essentially, fittingly, 'I can do no other.'" In his
> own words in *The Trumpet of Conscience*, Dr. King said, "It is
> many months now since I have found myself obliged by con-
> science to end my silence and to take a public stand against
> my country's war in Vietnam. The considerations which led
> me to that painful decision have not disappeared.[2]

Thus, Dr. Harding reminds us,

> By the end of 1967, King himself had moved beyond a narrow
> approach to the war in Vietnam and had long before rejected
> a single narrow focus on black rights in the United States. By
> the end of that crucial year, King was openly declaring that
> "the dispossessed of this nation—the poor, both white and
> Negro—live in a cruelly unjust society. They must organize
> a revolution against that injustice, not against the lives of
> . . . their fellow citizens, but against the structures through
> which the society is refusing . . . to lift the load of poverty."[3]

When King turned to this Nineveh, his vital proclamation and call to change was heard.

Nineveh—where God sends us even—or because—it seems so huge or hostile or hopeless or hard.

The ministry was Prathia Hall's Nineveh. In *Hands on the Freedom Plow: Personal Accounts by Women in SNCC*, Hall wrote of planning to go to law school "despite the war being waged in my consciousness against the compelling call to the ordained ministry, a terrifying prospect for me, since I knew almost no ordained women ministers who were taken seriously by the church."[4] In her first days as a SNCC (Student Nonviolent Coordinating Committee) volunteer in Albany, Georgia, she remembers, "It was of great interest to me that both Charles Sherrod and Charles Jones, the leaders of the project, were seminary graduates. I said very little about my own theological journey, however, since I was trying desperately to escape or evade the call to ministry."[5]

Thankfully, Prathia Hall eventually turned toward her Nineveh and became a pastor and professor of social ethics. Named by *Ebony* magazine as one of the nation's most outstanding African American women preachers, Prathia Hall was responsible for training many other black women preachers.

Nineveh—where God sends us even if, or because—it seems so huge or hostile or hopeless or hard.

What's your Nineveh? What are you being called to do that has made you want to run in the other direction? Have you turned your face toward it, or are you still headed in the other direction? Where has God called you that you'd rather not go? What is that place—that issue, task, challenge, or call—that is far outside your comfort zone but is precisely where God calls you to comfort the afflicted and afflict the comfortable? Where is the place God sends you *because* it is huge, hard, full of injustice, and important to God that it change?

Is your Nineveh something that seems too huge—the next strategy that's needed, the next project that is overwhelming, the task of trying to mobilize a denomination or state or nation?

Is your Nineveh something that seems too hostile—the "others" who don't share your values or who seem too different in region, race, or religion? Is it a sector you've given up on, a community that you've tried to avoid or where you've not felt welcome?

Is your Nineveh something that seems too hopeless or hard—changing a policy or program or practice, stopping altogether instead of just slowing the tide of violence or poverty or racism or incarceration or teen pregnancy?

What is your Nineveh? Where is God calling you that seems huge, hostile, hopeless, or hard?

Get Up and Go

Whatever our Nineveh is, God's call to Jonah—and to us—is the same: *get up, go at once, and proclaim my message.* We recall that after Jonah ran away from God's first call to go to Nineveh, he wound up on the ship for Tarshish. A storm overtook them, and he told the sailors—to their dismay—to throw him overboard. He spent three days in the belly of a great fish offering a hymn of surrender and thanksgiving to God before, at God's command, the fish vomited him upon the ground.

When my children were young, I read an article that gave the parenting advice to be the "broken record." When you tell your children to do something—say, clean up their toys—if they don't do it right away, you just repeat the instruction verbatim. You don't explain, you don't expound, you don't argue, you don't raise your voice, you don't give in. You just repeat it until they realize that the demand is not going to change and it is not going to go away, and so they finally do it. I think God may have read—or written—that article. Because God's command to Jonah the second time is the same as the first time:

> The word of the LORD came to Jonah a second time, saying, "Get up, go to Nineveh, that great city, and proclaim to it the message that I tell you."
> So Jonah set out and went to Nineveh, according to the word of the LORD. Now Nineveh was an exceedingly large city, a three days' walk across. Jonah began to go into the

city, going a day's walk. And he cried out, "Forty days more, and Nineveh shall be overthrown!"

(Jonah 3:1–4)

Whatever our Nineveh is, God's call to Jonah—and to us— is the same: get up, go at once, and proclaim my message. The Hebrew words for the instruction to "get up and go" are combined in an unusual way. The particular combination serves to reinforce the urgency and immediacy of the command, the need for movement. "Get up and go, go at once, go immediately. Go at once—go beyond your comfort zone; go beyond the 'usual suspects' and just 'preaching to the choir.' Get going: you're not going to get it done standing still, so get moving now."

The second part of the instruction is "Cry out," proclaim the message God gives us, proclaim justice, proclaim that the injustice must end. God told Jonah, "Cry out against [Nineveh]; for their wickedness has come up before me." Rabbi Abraham Heschel, in his book *The Prophets*, wrote, "All prophecy is one great exclamation: God is not indifferent to evil!" Rabbi Heschel continues, "[God] is always concerned. [God] is personally affected by what man does to man. [God] is a God of pathos. This is one of the meanings of the anger of God: the end of indifference!"[6]

What happens when we do get up, go to Nineveh, and proclaim God's message? Does it make a difference? In our Scripture passage, we hear what happened when Jonah went to Nineveh and proclaimed:

And the people of Nineveh believed God; they proclaimed a fast, and everyone, great and small, put on sackcloth.

When the news reached the king of Nineveh, he rose from his throne, removed his robe, covered himself with sackcloth, and sat in ashes. Then he had a proclamation made in Nineveh: "By the decree of the king and his nobles: No human being or animal, no herd or flock, shall taste anything. They shall not feed, nor shall they drink water. Human beings and animals shall be covered with sackcloth, and they

shall cry mightily to God. All shall turn from their evil ways and from the violence that is in their hands. Who knows? God may relent and change [God's] mind; [God] may turn from [God's] fierce anger, so that we do not perish."
When God saw what they did, how they turned from their evil ways, God changed [God's] mind about the calamity that [God] had said [God] would bring upon them; and [God] did not do it.

(Jonah 3:1:5–10)

Jonah's proclamation started a movement, a movement that began with the people who believed God. The movement involved all ages, "everyone, great and small" as they began a fast and put on sackcloth—symbolizing their repentance, their commitment to turn in a new direction.

The movement among the people created change at the highest political levels. When the news reached the king of Nineveh, he rose from his chair and turned in a new direction, removing the trappings of privilege and wearing the rags of repentance. And then he got together with the nobles and called for an end to the injustice they had been practicing, decreeing that "all shall turn from their evil ways and from the violence that is in their hands" (v. 8). Imagine a similar turn from the injustice of tax breaks for billionaires at the expense of babies, padding the pockets of the rich and leaving children in poverty. Imagine a turn from the evil of worrying more about the jobs of leaders than the jobs of the people. Imagine turning from the violence of building prisons rather than paths out of the pipeline and the violence of bailing out banks but leaving homes under water. Turn from all of this, saying, "I think I get it; if we do this—if we care for our children and invest in our future—it may be that we will not perish!" Imagine that leadership lightbulb going off: Could it be that practicing *justice* may secure a future of hope, as we won't suffer the inevitable repercussions of *injustice*?

When Jonah finally turned in a new direction, to Nineveh, the people turned in a new direction—away from evil. And when the people turned in a new direction, the political leadership turned in a new direction, and God turned in response from plans for judgment to mercy. Jonah found the task wasn't as huge, hostile, hopeless, or hard as he had imagined. But even if it had been, it was still where he was called to go.

Will it always be so easy? No. The outlandish and outsize details of the story (even the animals wore sackcloth) remind us that these are lessons painted with a broad and very colorful brush that we might see them more easily—while also pointing to the encompassing nature of God's care and vision for renewal. At the end of the book, the details of Jonah's sulking—because God's mercy on Nineveh made Jonah look like he had been mistaken—remind us that even when we are successful, there's always the temptation to be dissatisfied or disappointed, to worry more about how we look than how God looks. It leaves us with the challenge to embrace a God who forgives not only us but also those we see as enemies.

God sends us even if our Ninevehs look huge, hostile, hopeless, or hard because that's where we are needed—it is where injustice lies, and it matters to God that it change. It is where God needs us to start the movement that turns things around. And so we are called to arise, go with urgency to our own Ninevehs, and proclaim God's message to transform our communities and nation to ones that reflect God's intentions for love and justice. Where is your Nineveh? It's time to get going, knowing that with God nothing is too huge, too hostile, too hopeless, or too hard. Thanks be to God.

∼

Questions for Faithful Response

1. What is your Nineveh? What are you being called to do that has made you want to run the other direction?

2. Is your Nineveh something that seems too huge—the next strategy that's needed, the next project that is overwhelming, the task of trying to mobilize a denomination or state

or nation? How could you approach that Nineveh to make it more manageable?

3. Is your Nineveh something that seems too hostile—the "others" who don't share your values or who seem too different in region, race, or religion, or a place you've given up on, a community that you've tried to avoid or where you've not felt welcome? How could you approach the hostile Nineveh to create more receptivity?

4. Is your Nineveh something that seems too hopeless or hard—changing a policy or program or practice, stopping instead of just slowing the tide of violence or poverty or racism or incarceration or teen pregnancy? How could you sustain your hope and commitment while taking it on?

5. When in the past have you encountered a Nineveh? What happened? How did that experience affect your faith? How does it influence your response when you encounter new Ninevehs?

6. *Especially for parents and other caregivers:* Children often think of their parents as all-knowing and powerful. It may come as a surprise to them to hear about a time that you were daunted by a challenge that lay ahead—and a comfort to know that everyone, even grown-ups, face and can overcome feelings of anxiety at big challenges. Share your Nineveh experience with them in an age-appropriate way, and then invite them to talk about their own Ninevehs—times in the past or present when they have encountered a challenge that felt huge, hostile, or hard. Discuss the difference between expecting that God will always make things easy and the promise that God will be with us in the challenges.

Chapter Six

Team of Rivals

Isaiah 11

A shoot will grow up from the stump of Jesse;
  a branch will sprout from his roots.
The LORD's spirit will rest upon him,
  a spirit of wisdom and understanding,
  a spirit of planning and strength,
  a spirit of knowledge and fear of the LORD.
He will delight in fearing the LORD.
He won't judge by appearances,
  nor decide by hearsay.
He will judge the needy with righteousness,
  and decide with equity for those who suffer in the land.
He will strike the violent with the rod of his mouth;
  by the breath of his lips he will kill the wicked.
Righteousness will be the belt around his hips,
  and faithfulness the belt around his waist.
The wolf will live with the lamb,
  and the leopard will lie down with the young goat;
  the calf and the young lion will feed together,
  and a little child will lead them.

The cow and the bear will graze.
Their young will lie down together,
and a lion will eat straw like an ox.
A nursing child will play over the snake's hole;
toddlers will reach right over the serpent's den.
They won't harm or destroy anywhere on my holy mountain.
The earth will surely be filled with the knowledge of
the LORD,
just as the water covers the sea.

(Isa. 11:1–9 CEB)

Hollywood's Washington

It seems like whenever you flip on the TV around the holidays, you are likely to run across Jimmy Stewart in *It's a Wonderful Life*. A few days before one Christmas, however, when his face appeared on screen, it was instead in *Mr. Smith Goes to Washington*, and I found myself drawn in even though the movie was half over. I wound up watching until the end. His character, the idealistic rookie senator, was in the midst of a valiant filibuster, trying to advocate for justice over greed, truth and goodness over corruption, and concern for children over corporate interests. Mr. Smith was quoting from the Constitution, recalling the statue representing liberty on top of the Capitol dome and all she stood for. He talked about the children and the need to invest in their nurture and development as they will one day be filling the seats of power.

"There's no place out there for graft or greed or lies or compromise with human liberties," he said. "And if that's what the grown-ups have done to this world . . . we'd better . . . see what the kids can do."

His opponent, Senator Paine, had been waging a relentless effort to silence Mr. Smith so that he could satisfy a rich corporate interest instead of investing in the children. Mocking Mr. Smith for expecting supporters to rally in large numbers, Senator Paine calls for baskets of telegrams he had trumped up in opposition to Mr. Smith's efforts to win justice, telegraphs that one bystander calls "public opinion made to order."

At the same time as this action is going on in the Capitol building, children and other supporters of Mr. Smith are being violently silenced by Paine's henchmen.

When Mr. Smith sees these negative telegrams spilling out of the basket Paine had brought in, he seems momentarily defeated, ready to fold. Then he has a last resurgence of determination to, as he puts it, champion "lost causes." Mr. Smith reminds Mr. Paine that he once knew about fighting for lost causes—"the only causes worth fighting for, and [Mr. Paine] fought for them once . . . because of just one plain, simple rule, 'Love thy neighbor.' And in this world today, full of hatred, a man who knows that one rule has a great trust. . . . You fight for the lost causes harder than for any others. Yes, you'd even die for them, like a man we both know, Mr. Paine."

Mr. Smith faints at that point. His opponent disappears, and then a pistol shot is heard as Mr. Smith's opponent, in what appears to be a failed suicide attempt, cries in despair because what was said was true—he was guilty and should be expelled from office. At this point Mr. Smith's sweetheart and supporter lets out the movie's last word: "Yippee!"

Congress's Washington

If you had grabbed the remote that night just before Christmas and switched over from the AMC movie channel to C-Span, you would have seen a whole other story playing out. The C-Span coverage of the closing hours of the health reform debate in the Senate didn't include any last-minute changes of heart from those who had been most opposed to the hopes of health-care reform. No senator cried out that he'd been wrong, that the health-insurance giants of his home state had his ear more than the uninsured children there. Not a single Republican shouted, "Aye" when it came time for his or her vote. There was no great reversal, no dramatic vindication for the champions of the children, the champions of what others consider lost causes. No repentance for greed, or callousness, or concerns about reelection that had trumped concern for the littlest. There may have been relief that we had gotten this far, but there wasn't anything that prompted a huge, Hollywood "yippee" of victory.

Central Washington

If you had taken up the remote control one last time, that night just before Christmas, you might have had a third glimpse of what can happen when opponents face each other. This scene didn't play out in *Mr. Smith Goes to Washington* on the AMC movie channel. It didn't play out in the U.S. Capitol on C-Span. Instead it came to us from ESPN in a top-ten round-up of the best moments in sports of the past year.

Picture a softball field in Washington—not the Washington of the movie or the real Congress, but the state of Washington, just about as far as you can get from Washington, DC. The ballfield was tucked away in a small town over the mountains from Seattle. There were bleachers for only three hundred people, and two-thirds of the seats were empty. Despite the modest setting, it was the biggest game of the year—or for some, of their lives—for the two college teams that faced off. This game would determine who went on to play for the division championship. For the college seniors, it was the climax of their careers.

Playing for the Central Washington team was Mallory Holtman—a powerhouse who was famous for her home runs and numerous records—playing on her home turf. On Western Oregon's team was little Sara Tucholsky, who had never hit a home run. As she came to the plate, she endured the taunts of her opponents' fans. ESPN's Graham Hayes reported that "a few overzealous fans [were] heckling an easy target."[1] Two of Sara's teammates were already on base, and the game was still scoreless. "You don't have a chance," hecklers might have called out. "You've struck out before; you'll strike out again." The nasty shouts and name calling continued.

Sara tried not to pay attention to her mockers and instead focus on the pitch coming to her. She didn't swing at the first one—it was a strike. Then the next pitch left the pitcher's hand, and she took a swing. As soon as her bat connected with the ball, she knew it was headed over the fence. Before that crack of the ball, she had never hit a home run and in fact had only gotten three hits the whole season. "And in that respect," later wrote Hayes, "her hitting heroics would have made for a pleasing, if familiar, story line on their own: an unsung player steps up in one of her final games and lifts her team's postseason chances. But it was what happened [next] . . . that proved unforgettable."

Sara had indeed hit the ball out of the ballpark. Her coach high-fived Sara's two teammates who had been on base as each crossed home plate. Then, the coach looked up and wondered, "Where's Sara?" She looked across the field and saw Sara in a heap in the dirt just beyond first base.

It turned out that in her excitement at the prospect of her first-ever home run, Sara had overshot first base without tagging it. She had turned quickly to go back to tag first base before going on and in that sudden pivot had torn her ACL (anterior cruciate ligament)—a devastating injury that dropped her to the ground and rendered her helpless to move forward on her own.

Her two teammates had already passed home. Sara was the only one on her team left on the field of play. She lay helpless "a few feet from first base and a long way from home."

The umpire ruled that no one on her team could help the injured girl—not her coach, not her teammates. If they touched her, she would be out. Even if they replaced her with a healthy runner, it would have disqualified the hit from being a home run. Her replacement would have been left all the way back on first base instead of crossing home plate for the third run that Sara's home run should have earned.[2]

"And right then," [Sara's coach] said, "I heard, 'Excuse me, would it be OK if we carried her around and she touched each bag?'" The voice belonged to Mallory Holtman, a four-year starter who owns just about every major offensive record there is to claim in Central Washington's record book. Now, with her own opportunity to play for the championship for the first and only time very much hinging on the outcome of the game—her final game at home—she stepped up to help a player she knew only as an opponent for four years.

"Honestly, it's one of those things that I hope anyone would do it for me," Holtman said. "She hit the ball over the fence. She's a senior; it's her last year. . . . I don't know, it's just one of those things. . . . But I think anyone who knew that we could touch her would have offered to do it, just because it's the right thing to do. She was obviously in agony."

While it seemed obvious to Mallory that it was the right thing to do—to help her opponent, to respond to someone in agony who couldn't make it home by herself—given the high stakes, the fever pitch of competition, and the expectations of the partisan fans who had been yelling in the stands. . . . I'm not as sure as she that just anyone would have done the same thing.

Mallory called over another of her teammates, shortstop Liz Wallace, and together they picked Sara up out of the dirt and carried her between them, stopping at first base so her uninjured, left foot could touch the base, and then slowly carrying her toward second base, pausing so Sara's foot could touch that base, and then carrying her on to third.

During this, what the sportswriter called "the longest and most crowded home run trot in the game's history," the three women were accompanied by a standing ovation from the fans—the ones who had moments earlier been heckling Sara, rabid fans of their own team to whom it had never occurred that there was another way.

As the crowd of Central Washington fans cheered, Mallory and Liz, carrying Sara, finally reached home plate where they touched Sara down so that she could score the third run against their own team, and then Mallory and Liz handed Sara over into the arms of her waiting teammates.

Then Mallory and Liz "returned to their positions and tried to win the game," writes sportswriter Hayes, who further comments,

> Hollywood would have a difficult time deciding how such a script should end, whether to leave [Sara's] home run as

the decisive blow or reward the selfless actions of her opponents. Reality has less room for such philosophical quandaries. [Mallory's team] Central Washington did rally for two runs in the bottom of the second—runs that might have tied the game had [Sara's coach] been forced to replace [Sara]—but Western Oregon—[Sara's team]—held on for a 4-2 win. But unlike a movie, the credits didn't roll after the final out, and the story that continues has little to do with those final scores.

The actions of the young player Mallory had a lasting impact on the adults—from the fans, to the umpire who still tears up even years later recalling that game, to Sara's coach, who says, "It kept everything in perspective and the fact that we're never bigger than the game. It was such a lesson that we learned—that it's not all about winning. And we forget that, because as coaches, we're always trying to get to the top. We forget that. But I will never, ever forget this moment. It's changed me, and I'm sure it's changed my players."

Mallory continues to downplay the extraordinary nature of her actions and believes that it is what anyone else in her situation would have done. But, concludes Hayes, "she appreciates the knowledge that while the results of Saturday's game and her senior season soon will fade into the dust and depth of old media guides and Internet archives, the story of what happened in her final game at home will live on far longer."

From a little ballfield in Washington State to the mountain top that Isaiah envisioned, there is a glimpse of our world as God intends, when doing the right thing trumps keeping score, when you can lose and still win, and where justice for the poor and meek create at last a world in which old enemies can coexist in peace—with a child leading the way.

And I think of the other Washington, our Capitol, and I think about what lies ahead for children as we see them endure the undeserved pain of poverty and other harms and know that they need our help. Will Congress and our nation remain deadlocked in old oppositions while the child lies injured and suffering—stranded on first base with no way to get all the way home on her own? Or will this finally be the time that we succeed at creating justice? Might it even be the time that old opponents do the unexpected, let go of the concern about their own team's win, about the score-keeping, and do the right thing—assist the injured and the suffering and take them up in their arms to assure that they make it all the way home? Let us work and pray that it may be so. Amen.

~

Questions for Faithful Response

1. How do you feel about the prospects of Congress and our nation moving beyond "gridlock" and old oppositions? What do you think could make a difference?

2. When have you seen longtime opponents do the unexpected? What creates such an opportunity, and what works against it?

3. When have you seen a young person modeling a new and unexpected response to injustice that changed adults' old ways of thinking and acting?

4. Mallory believed that her actions were what anyone in her circumstance would have done. What do you think brings out the best in people? What is a situation in which you could "lose" but still win because you had done the right thing by seeking justice?

5. Is Isaiah's vision too unrealistic to have any application to our world here and now, or is there a truth, wisdom, or application you take from it? If so, what is it?

6. *Especially for parents and other caregivers:* Talk with children about Isaiah's vision of the peaceable kingdom. Perhaps you will want to draw pictures together of what it looks like. Then talk together about today—are there people who don't get along because they think they are opposites or enemies? How can children help lead the way to show others how to get along?

Chapter Seven

Certainly Not

Acts 16

When they had brought [Paul and Silas] before the magistrates, they said, "These men are disturbing our city; they
are Jews and are advocating customs that are not lawful for
us as Romans to adopt or observe." The crowd joined in
attacking them, and the magistrates had them stripped of
their clothing and ordered them to be beaten with rods. After
they had given them a severe flogging, they threw them into
prison and ordered the jailer to keep them securely. Following these instructions, he put them in the innermost cell and
fastened their feet in the stocks.

About midnight Paul and Silas were praying and singing hymns to God, and the prisoners were listening to
them. Suddenly there was an earthquake, so violent that the
foundations of the prison were shaken; and immediately all
the doors were opened and everyone's chains were unfas-
tened. When the jailer woke up and saw the prison doors
wide open, he drew his sword and was about to kill himself,
since he supposed that the prisoners had escaped. But Paul
shouted in a loud voice, "Do not harm yourself, for we are
all here." The jailer called for lights, and rushing in, he fell
down trembling before Paul and Silas. Then he brought

them outside and said, "Sirs, what must I do to be saved?" They answered, "Believe on the Lord Jesus, and you will be saved, you and your household." They spoke the word of the Lord to him and to all who were in his house. At the same hour of the night he took them and washed their wounds; then he and his entire family were baptized without delay. He brought them up into the house and set food before them; and he and his entire household rejoiced that he had become a believer in God.

When morning came, the magistrates sent the police, saying, "Let those men go." And the jailer reported the message to Paul, saying, "The magistrates sent word to let you go; therefore come out now and go in peace." But Paul replied, "They have beaten us in public, uncondemned, men who are Roman citizens, and have thrown us into prison; and now are they going to discharge us in secret? Certainly not! Let them come and take us out themselves." The police reported these words to the magistrates, and they were afraid when they heard that they were Roman citizens; so they came and apologized to them. And they took them out and asked them to leave the city.

(Acts 16:20–39)

"Certainly not," said Paul, when the Roman magistrates tried to hide their unjust treatment of Paul and Silas. What happens when we say, "Certainly not"? What kind of transformative power is there when we stand on principle and reject the half justice, the inadequate response, the expectation of complicity in or silence about injustice, or the false freedom with strings attached?

What happens when we say, "Certainly not" and then assert what should be done, what justice demands? While somewhat obscured in English translations of this Scripture passage, immediately following the declaration translated "Certainly not" comes the Greek word *alla*, a strong word asserting, "But rather." What happens when we with Paul say, "Certainly not!" and then offer a strong assertion of what justice *does* demand?

In 1963 SNCC (Student Nonviolent Coordinating Committee) field secretary Sam Block stood his ground with his own "Certainly not." It was in Greenwood, Mississippi—just down the road from the town in LeFlore County where Emmett Till had been viciously murdered. Greenwood was as oppressive a town as just about any—home to the state's White Citizens' Council, which made it an especially dangerous and difficult place to organize voter registration drives and other mobilizations for the civil rights movement. One day an anonymous caller warned that the new office space that SNCC had finally been able to rent was going to be destroyed. Sure enough, arsonists set a fire that burned four black businesses adjacent to the SNCC office, but the arsonists failed to burn the SNCC office—their intended target.

When Sam Block rightly described the fire as arson at a public meeting, he was arrested for "statements calculated to breach the peace." It was his seventh arrest for civil disobedience in Greenwood.

More than one hundred black protesters showed up at City Hall on the day of Sam's trial. He was sentenced to six months in jail and a $500 fine. The judge offered to suspend the sentence if Sam would agree to stop working for SNCC, give up the voter registration project, and leave town. "Judge," Mr. Block replied, "I ain't gonna do none of that." Leave town and abandon voter registration and mass mobilization? Certainly not. Block's "Certainly not!" inspired a mass meeting of 250 people that same night—it was the largest number of people to turn out for a movement meeting in Greenwood up to that time.

That January in 1964, Ella Baker spoke at a planning meeting strategizing about Freedom Day in Hattiesburg, Mississippi, "holding the crowd," as historian Howard Zinn put it, "with a vision beyond the immediate." Ella Baker spoke to the positive vision of what must replace that which we stand against. She proclaimed, "Even if segregation is gone, we will still need to be free; we will still have to see that everyone has a job. Even if we can all vote, but if people are still hungry, we will not be free. . . . Singing alone is not enough; we need schools and learning. . . . Remember," she concluded, "we are not fighting for the freedom of the Negro alone, but for the freedom of the human spirit, a larger freedom that encompasses all mankind."[1]

Some twenty years later, "Certainly not! But rather . . ." rang out from a prison cell in South Africa. While much of the world focused on one goal, freeing Nelson Mandela, the prisoner himself held a broader view of what justice required. President Botha, like those who had thrown Paul in jail, was increasingly desperate to get the prisoner off his hands but wasn't willing to end the injustice or admit his own guilt. He made an offer of a conditional release that required Mandela to renounce the African National Congress (ANC) and its goals for a free South Africa. Mandela wrote later, "By my reckoning, it was the sixth conditional offer the government had made for my release in the past ten years."[2] *Six times* he refused offers of release that came with conditions he would not accept.

In words that had to be read by another since he was still silenced, Mandela responded publicly to Botha's offering, saying,

> I am surprised at the conditions that the government wants to impose on me. . . . Let [Botha] renounce violence. Let him say that he will dismantle apartheid. Let him unban the people's organization, the African National Congress. Let him free all who have been imprisoned, banished, or exiled for their opposition to apartheid. Let him guarantee free political activity so that people may decide who will govern them.
>
> I cherish my own freedom dearly, but I care even more for your freedom. Too many have died since I went to prison. Too many have suffered for the love of freedom. I owe it to their widows, to their orphans, to their mothers, and to their fathers who have grieved and wept for them. Not only I have suffered during these long, lonely, wasted years. I am not less life-loving than you are. But I cannot sell my birthright, nor am I prepared to sell the birthright of the people to be free. . . .

What freedom am I being offered while the organization of the people remains banned? . . . What freedom am I being offered when my very South African citizenship is not respected?
Only free men can negotiate. Prisoners cannot enter into contracts. . . . I cannot and will not give any undertaking at a time when I and you, the people, are not free. Your freedom and mine cannot be separated. I will return.[3]

Leave prison when the people remained captive in apartheid? Certainly not. Mandela's "Certainly not!" was heard round the world and intensified pressure for a full dismantling of apartheid and genuine freedom for Mandela.

We are called to stand with those who have already declared and must continue to declare, "Certainly not" to the half justice, the easy way out, and the inadequate response, and we are called to demand publicly that instead justice be done right, that freedom be realized fully and fairly.

We're called to say, "Certainly not" when the open door doesn't represent real freedom but an inadequate response. I think about young people who have served their time in detention centers in Los Angeles. A policy brief by the Children's Defense Fund-California and the UCLA Luskin School of Public Affairs, *Reforming the Nation's Largest Juvenile Justice System*, found that most juveniles who are released from long-term secure placement in Los Angeles County were not successfully reintegrating into their communities.[4] It doesn't help to throw open the prison door and tell children to go on their way when we haven't put in place the secure footing they need to walk back into their communities and not get tripped up again. Children are still captive if they don't have health and mental health services, aren't helped to get back into school, and are thrown back into the same violent neighborhoods that got them into trouble in the first place. We can't just say, "You're free now; leave town quietly," as they said to Paul.

Marian Wright Edelman met with the Los Angeles county supervisor to say, "Certainly not!" Just sending young people out of detention this way is not sufficient, and it is not just; you have to do this the right way, with justice. The young people require services and supports that meaningfully engage them in school, employment, and community life if they are to successfully exit the cradle-to-prison pipeline and enter the pipeline to college and work. When we say, "Certainly not!" it creates pressure for real justice and a better response.

I think about the children who, like Paul and Silas, weren't condemned—they weren't charged and convicted, just arrested—and yet found themselves in baggy brown jumpsuits in the intake center of the notorious Spofford juvenile detention center in New York. Visiting there with a group of child advocates pressuring authorities to close the facility, we heard the intake officer call a child's personal and family information the child's "pedigree"—as though the child were a dog rather than a person. The children were treated as if they were guilty and already convicted. CDF and other child advocates stood with those children and declared, "Certainly not!"—it's not enough to let them go eventually . . . they never should have been in this prison setting in the first place. We need to treat them like the children and citizens they are. Youth advocates and community organizers kept saying it until Spofford was closed forever in 2011. "'They brought the gate down [on the closed facility], put the padlock on and there were church bells ringing,' said Reverend Ruben Austria, executive director of South Bronx–based Community Connections for Youth. 'It gave me a feeling of great joy. There is still more work to be done, but today was a victory.'"[5]

As some in Congress try to undo the health insurance our children need and deserve, we must declare, "Certainly not!" Together, we must insist that every child has a healthy start with the accessible, affordable preventive care and treatment they need.

When Congress makes budget decisions that don't include sufficient funding for early childhood investments, youth development, and violence prevention, we must declare, "Certainly not!" We must insist instead on strong early childhood development for every child, Head Start for every eligible child, excellent schools with high expectations, and the preparation and support children need for a future of promise and success.

We need to be the strong voices who keep standing up to the wealthy and to businesses and say, "Certainly not!" to more tax breaks for them, to cuts to children's programs, and to deals that give our children crumbs while the wealthy take the cake. Together we must insist, instead, that every child deserves a fair start, with investments that help parents earn a living wage and safety nets that protect children from the worst effects of poverty.

When the NRA leadership and politicians in their debt block sensible gun-safety policies, we must declare, "Certainly not!" Instead, we must raise a voice that says instead that every child deserves a safe start with sensible gun-safety measures to reduce the deadly toll of gun accidents, suicides, and homicides that take the lives of the equivalent of a classroom full of children every three days in our nation, and we must press on until such measures are finally in place.

We're called to say, "Certainly not!" to compromise that leaves injustice in place and unchallenged. We're called to say, "Certainly not" when there is a principle at stake, when the truth is more important than the "win." Others may cave to unjust compromise, but children need to know that they can count on us to be the ones who stand up and say, "Certainly not."

When we look back to Paul and Silas's experience, we see hints of what may renew and strengthen us in our determination to say, "Certainly not" when the occasion demands it. They had spent the night in prayer and singing—and we know how central that is to any justice movement and to our own lives. Paul had seen God's earth-shaking capacity to create change in our world—and we can trust that even now God is using us to shake things up, throw open prison doors, and loose chains. Paul may even have been strengthened in his capacity to declare, "Certainly not" by the experience of his jailor—a former oppressor, a former opponent, a former part of the system—who had a change of heart, a conversion experience. When we know that we can, by God's grace, change hearts, minds, and perspectives, we are encouraged to stand up and demand full, real justice and true, meaningful freedom. And we know that Paul and those with him had just broken bread together—which surely strengthened him in his demand for real justice.

The transformative possibilities that arise when we say, "Certainly not!" were described by Shane Claiborne, a founding partner of the Simple Way, in his book *The Irresistible Revolution: Living as an Ordinary Radical.* Claiborne wrote,

> Philadelphia had begun to pass anti-homeless legislation, making it illegal to sleep in the parks, illegal to ask for money, illegal to lie down on the sidewalks. They even chose to implement it on Dr. King's birthday! Ironically, the reason for many of these laws was Love Park, which is a historic site in Philly known as a great place for skateboarding (which was also made illegal). Love Park was a place where homeless folks hung out. It was visible, safe, and central. Folks knew they could go there to give out food or clothing to people on the street. We used to go there back when we were in college, and there are some nice steam vents that kept people (and some big rats) warm. One of the city's boldest moves was passing an ordinance that banned all food from the park. Specifically, it reads, "All persons must cease and desist from distributing food." And they began fining those of us who continued to share food. We started wondering what in the world it meant to love our neighbors as ourselves when they were being jailed for sleeping and eating. As St. Augustine said, "An unjust law is no law at all." What did it mean to submit to authority and yet uphold God's law of love? Either we had to invite them into our home (which reached capacity), or we wanted to be out with them, in solidarity. So we threw a party in Love Park.
>
> About a hundred of us gathered in Love Park with homeless friends. We worshiped, sang, and prayed. Then we served communion, which was illegal. But with clergy and city officials there supporting us, and with police and the media surrounding us, we celebrated communion. Most of the police sat back and watched, not daring to arrest

anyone, especially during communion. Then we continued the "breaking of the bread" by bringing in pizzas. It was a love feast, and then we slept overnight in the park with our homeless friends. We did that week after week, with the police watching over us and the media standing by. And then one night after worship, as we slept under the "Love" sign which we had covered with a big question mark, the police circled the park and arrested all of us. Not the best wake-up call. We were taken to jail in handcuffs. But over and over, many of us slept out, and over and over, we were arrested, though sometimes the police were sympathetic and agreed that we should not be arrested for sleeping. A bunch of bigwig lawyers even called, offering to represent us. We were very thankful and invited them to come and support us, but we decided to be represented by a homeless friend, who wouldn't be able to have fancy lawyers if he were alone. So our buddy Fonz agreed to be our spokesperson.

As we stood before the judge, I wore a shirt that read, "Jesus was homeless." The judge asked me to step forward and I did.

He read my shirt aloud and said, "Hmm. I didn't know that."

I said, "Yes sir, in the Scriptures Jesus says that 'foxes have holes and birds have nests but the Son of Man has no place to lay his head.'"

The judge paused pensively and said, "You guys might stand a chance."

And we did.

Before we went to court, we read all of the Scriptures where Jesus warns the disciples that they will be dragged before courts and into jails, and they had new meaning for us. He warned them not to worry about what to say, so we didn't. When the time came for us to testify, Fonz stood up in court and said, "Your Honor, we think these laws are wrong." We said, "Amen. What he said."

The district attorney had her stuff together. She was not joking around. We faced numerous charges, jail time, thousands of dollars in fines, and hours and hours of community service. (Imagine that!)

The judge said to the court, "What is in question here is not whether these folks broke the law; that is quite clear. What is in question is the constitutionality of the law."

The DA shot back, "The constitutionality of the law is not before this court." And the DA threw her papers on the table.

The judge retorted, "The constitutionality of the law is before every court. Let me remind the court that if it weren't for people who broke unjust laws, we wouldn't have the freedom that we have. We'd still have slavery. That's the story of this country, from the Boston Tea Party to the civil rights movement. These people are not criminals; they are freedom fighters. I find them all not guilty, on every charge."

The papers called it a "Revolutionary Court Decision." And the judge asked us for a "Jesus was homeless" T-shirt.

We caught a glimpse of what Paul and Silas saw as they sang and prayed in that jail cell until "the prison doors flew open and everyone's chains came loose (Acts 16:26)."[6]

In sending Jesus, God declared God's own "Certainly not"— shall sin have the last word? Certainly not! Shall death have the last word? Certainly not! The first are first, and the last are left out? Certainly not! God's "but rather . . ." in Jesus declared that we are fully and freely forgiven, invited into a life of abundant joy and justice, community, and communion in which love and only love has the last word. Thanks be to God.

~

Questions for Faithful Response

1. What do you think helps you, or could help you, stand strong and declare, "Certainly not" to injustice and unfair compromise? What role do prayer, singing, community,

and Communion have in strengthening you for justice work?

2. Paul may even have been strengthened in his capacity to declare, "Certainly not" when his jailor—a former oppressor, a former opponent, a former part of the system—had a change of heart, a conversion experience. Have you ever been strengthened in your own advocacy by an opponent's change of heart?

3. The judge in Shane Claiborne's encounter was startled to think of Jesus as a homeless person. What gets in the way of seeing Jesus in people in difficult circumstances? What could help us identify Jesus with and in those who suffer and struggle the most?

4. How have we "domesticated" or "airbrushed" Jesus? What difference would it make if we saw him once again as countercultural, disruptive, unsettling, and unafraid to break unjust or unethical rules and laws?

5. The implicit "but rather" in the passage emphasizes the just alternative to the injustice that is being resisted. How do you see the role or importance of putting forth positive proposals for change in our work to resist injustice? What is your vision for the positive "but rather" that would replace the injustice against which we stand?

6. **Especially for parents and other caregivers:** Talk with children about compromising and standing firm. What are some situations when compromising is a good thing to do (for example, deciding which game to play with a friend)? What are some situations when standing firm and saying "no!" to something is a good thing to do (such as telling a lie or hurting someone's feelings on purpose)? What difference does it make when we offer a different, better alternative? With older children, talk about the different actions that people can take to change an unjust law or rule.

Chapter Eight

Confusion in the Valley of Vision

Isaiah 22

The oracle concerning the valley of vision.

What do you mean that you have gone up,
    all of you, to the housetops,
you that are full of shoutings,
    tumultuous city, exultant town?
Your slain are not slain by the sword,
    nor are they dead in battle.
Your rulers have all fled together;
    they were captured without the use of a bow.
All of you who were found were captured,
    though they had fled far away.
Therefore I said:
Look away from me,
    let me weep bitter tears;
do not try to comfort me
    for the destruction of my beloved people.

For the Lord GOD of hosts has a day
    of tumult and trampling and confusion
    in the valley of vision,

> a battering down of walls
>   and a cry for help to the mountains.
> Elam bore the quiver
>   with chariots and cavalry,
>   and Kir uncovered the shield.
> Your choicest valleys were full of chariots,
>   and the cavalry took their stand at the gates.
> He has taken away the covering of Judah.

On that day you looked to the weapons of the House of the Forest, and you saw that there were many breaches in the city of David, and you collected the waters of the lower pool. You counted the houses of Jerusalem, and you broke down the houses to fortify the wall. You made a reservoir between the two walls for the water of the old pool. But you did not look to him who did it, or have regard for him who planned it long ago.

> In that day the Lord God of hosts
>   called to weeping and mourning,
>   to baldness and putting on sackcloth;
> but instead there was joy and festivity,
>   killing oxen and slaughtering sheep,
>   eating meat and drinking wine.
> "Let us eat and drink,
>   for tomorrow we die."
> The Lord of hosts has revealed himself in my ears:
> Surely this iniquity will not be forgiven you until you die,
>   says the Lord God of hosts.
>   (Isa. 22:1–14)

It was a time of tumult and trampling and confusion in the Valley of Vision. The community was under siege—surrounded by forces that would harm them, impoverish and starve them, let their children die. If ever there was a time that the community needed to hold fast to God and rely on God's grace and strength to guide them, strengthen them, hold them together, this was it.

But God was the last thing on their minds. No, it was a time of tumult, trampling, and confusion in the Valley of Vision. The leadership fled—abdicated their responsibility for safeguarding the most vulnerable of the people. Instead, the leaders hightailed it for the hills. The remaining adults started scrambling for weapons, heading for the royal armory—the House of the Forest—where the weapons were stashed. Panicking at the breaches in the walls, they started repossessing some of the houses, tearing them down to try to fill the breaches with the wreckage of these former homes. I imagine it wasn't the houses of the most wealthy and powerful that got torn down to use for scrap wood but the houses of the least powerful families. They pooled old, fetid water, hoping it would do. In the mad rush, there was trampling—it was surely over the youngest, oldest, and sickest who couldn't get out of the way in time.

Rather than sober reflection and mourning, they turned to distraction, saying, "Let us eat and drink and be merry, for tomorrow we die." In the panicked scramble, it didn't occur to anyone to pray or seek God's guidance for this desperate time.

And then it was over—the siege ended, and the enemy withdrew. The leadership was captured, defenseless. Did the community weep over their slain children, reflect on what they could have done differently, and belatedly turn to God in prayer and confession, pleading for guidance and seeking a new vision? No. They had forgotten God during the siege, and they forgot God still in the aftermath.

The people whooped it up while God wept. There was death and desolation throughout the countryside—the "covering of Judah"—but those who escaped turned from death to distraction, with exultant shouting. Having stared death in the face, rather than living with sober, renewed purpose, they decided to party away the pain.

They turned to wine to forget, but God did not forget and forgive what the people did not even recognize as sin. Without repenting—turning in a new direction—they could not be saved from their death-dealing, dead-end ways.

There was indeed tumult and trampling and confusion in the Valley of Vision during the siege, but they had lost their vision and their way long before the external enemy forces surrounded them. This Valley of Vision is none other than Hinnom or the place that Jeremiah would refer to as Topeth—the notorious site of child sacrifice in the Bible. Yes, there was confusion in the Valley of Vision, where children were sacrificed on altars of the adults' making.

In Hebrew, the place would also be referred to as *ge-hinnon* or *Gehenna*, that is, Hell. *Surely hell is that place where children are sacrificed, vision is confused, and God is forgotten—where God alone has the heart to weep for the loss of God's beloved.*

There was a time when this community had heard God's vision for them. In the Valley of Vision, at one time they had heard God's vision for them as recounted by the prophet Isaiah:

> The wolf shall live with the lamb,
>   the leopard shall lie down with the kid,
> the calf and the lion and the fatling together,
>   and a little child shall lead them.
> The cow and the bear shall graze,
>   their young shall lie down together,
>   and the lion shall eat straw like the ox.
> The nursing child shall play over threshold of the asp,
>   and the weaned child shall put its hand on the adder's den.
> They will not hurt or destroy on all my holy mountain,
>   for the earth will be full of the knowledge of the LORD
>   as the waters cover the sea.
>
> (Isa. 11:6–9)

Yes, it was a valley that at one time had understood God's vision, before child sacrifice, siege, trampling, tumult, and confusion had overtaken them in the Valley of Vision. And so God wept, knowing that the end was near. A people cannot last long who sacrifice their children, lose their vision, and forget God. In little more than one hundred years, the nation of Judah would be no more, scattered in exile.

Is There Confusion in Our Valley of Vision?

Does it feel to you like we are once again experiencing tumult, trampling, and confusion in the Valley of Vision? How else to explain national priorities that put billionaires before babies? How else to explain trampling the hopes and dreams of children under the heavy boot of military spending or the casual crush of zero-tolerance discipline policies that have kindergarteners handcuffed instead of sent to the principal's office? There is confusion in the Valley of Vision when we protect Bushmaster assault weapons instead of babies, magazine clips instead of mothers. There is confusion in the Valley of Vision when we incarcerate rather than educate our children of color. There is confusion in the Valley of Vision when 14.5 million children in our rich nation live in poverty. Yes, there is confusion in the Valley of Vision, and God weeps while our nation parties. God calls for sackcloth, and we go shopping at Saks. God despairs, and we look for distraction.

How is our nation responding to this time of calamity, when our communities are under siege? Has our leadership, too, headed for the hills, fleeing responsibility to lead in times of crisis? Are we too looking to weapons—from a bloated military budget to weapons on the shelves at Walmart, or, heaven help us, to teachers who are armed? Are our families also losing their homes as the most economically vulnerable are somehow left to fill the breaches in our national walls? Are we, too, desperate for distraction, preferring reality TV to reality while we eat, drink, and make merry? Do we as a nation continue to ignore God and God's intentions for life together marked by justice and peace that would provide lasting security? Yes, there is confusion in the Valley of Vision, and God weeps.

Another Way

Is there another way? What does it look like when a community *doesn't* lose its vision when under siege? In 1347, during the Hundred Years War, King Edward III of England lay siege to the

French town of Calais. The strongly fortified town had refused to surrender, and so the English prepared to starve them out. They built houses around the perimeter of Calais and had supplies shipped from England so that they could eat while those within starved. And then they waited, waited for the people trapped inside the barricaded town to surrender. As the siege wore on, the English queen, Philippa, joined her husband, King Edward, in camp.

The citizens of Calais waited to be rescued by their leader, King Philippe VI. Sir Jean, the governor of the besieged Calais, wrote to King Phillipe, "We have eaten everything, even the cats, and dogs, and horses, and there is nothing left for us but to die of hunger unless you come soon." King Philippe responded, leading his army toward Calais, but after a few losing skirmishes with the English forces encamped there, he left without saving his people.

The people of Calais were running out of food, water, strength, and hope. Finally, their governor raised the white flag of surrender on the town's battlements. King Edward sent emissaries to confirm that the town would surrender. The governor of Calais responded that he would give up the town—its buildings and belongings, castles and treasures—in exchange for the English king's sparing the lives of the people. The English king, however, refused, asserting, "the only grace he must expect from me is that six of the principal citizens of Calais march out of the town, with bare heads and feet, with ropes round their necks, and the keys of the town and castle in their hands. These six persons shall be at my absolute disposal [to be executed], and the remainder of the inhabitants pardoned."[1] The weak, desperate, and despairing citizens of Calais were assembled in the marketplace, and the Governor informed them of the English king's demand.

Calais's wealthiest merchant, Eustace de St. Pierre, spoke first, saying,

> "Gentlemen, it would be a great shame to allow so many people to starve to death, if there were any way of preventing it. And it would be highly pleasing to Our Lord if anyone could save them from such a fate." He continued, "I

have such faith and trust in gaining pardon and grace from Our Lord if I die in the attempt, that I will put myself forward as the first. I will willingly go out in my shirt, bareheaded and barefoot, with a halter [noose] around my neck and put myself at the mercy of the King of England." Five more prominent merchants stepped forward: John Daire, James Wisant and his brother Peter, and two others.[2]

The six merchants, also known as Burghers, left the city to turn themselves over to the English king. They expected to be killed, which was what King Edward fully intended to do. His wife, Queen Philippa, however, was pregnant and feared that killing the burghers would be a bad omen for the child she carried. The mother-to-be persuaded her husband not to kill the six men who had offered themselves up. And so it was that the burghers, who had been prepared to die for the sake of their community, were spared.

Compare that kind of leadership, in which the wealthy and powerful offer themselves up and sacrifice themselves to end the suffering of the community and its children, to what we saw in recent years as our nation approached the so-called "fiscal cliff." Some leaders in Congress acted as if their first duty was to keep the wealthy and powerful barricaded within the citadel of Congress, protected from any demands of sacrifice, the suffering of children and the poor be damned. There is confusion in the Valley of Vision when privilege and power is seen as a right to protection rather than as a responsibility to protect those without privilege and power.

In the late 1800s, sculptor Auguste Rodin was commissioned by the town of Calais to sculpt a monument in tribute to these heroes. They expected something traditional and heroic set high upon a pedestal, lauding the courage of the leaders and placing Eustace de Saint-Pierre—the first to volunteer—at the pinnacle as the most important and famous. To the town's dismay, they got something very different—more human than conventionally heroic and treating all six of the Burghers as equal in status. The monument shows the men as they are leaving the city, prepared to die. Each of the men sculpted shows a different emotion on his face and in his posture. They are linked as a group in their commitment to the cause, to the sacrifice, yet distinct in their individual experiences of the moment. One looks back; another, down: yet another bends his head into his hands while still another faces forward. Fear, doubt, resolve, despair, and resignation are reflected in their unique expressions. Rodin explained:

> "I did not hesitate to make them as thin and as weak as possible. If, in order to respect some academic convention or other, I had tried to show bodies that were still agreeable to look at, I would have betrayed my subject. These people, having passed through the privations of a long siege, no longer have anything but skin on their bones. The more frightful my representation of them, the more people should praise me for knowing how to show the truth of history. I have not shown them grouped in a triumphant apotheosis; such glorification of their heroism would not have corresponded to anything real. On the contrary, I have, as it were, threaded them one behind the other, because in the indecision of the last inner combat which ensues, between their devotion to their cause and their fear of dying, each of them is isolated in front of his conscience. They are still questioning themselves to know if they have the strength to accomplish the supreme sacrifice—their soul pushes them onward, but their feet refuse to walk."[3]

The committee that had commissioned the monument objected, writing, "This is not the way we envisaged our glorious citizens going to the camp of the King of England. Their defeated postures offend our religion."[4]

Rodin did not want the sculpture elevated on a pedestal. He wanted the figures to be at the same level as those who viewed the sculpture. He explained:

> I did not want a pedestal for these figures. I wanted them to be placed on, even affixed to, the paving stones of the square

in front of the Hôtel de Ville in Calais so that it looked as if
they were leaving in order to go to the enemy camp. In this
way they would have been, as it were, mixed with the daily
life of the town: passersby would have elbowed them, and
they would have felt through this contact the emotion of the
living past in their midst; they would have said to themselves:
"Our ancestors are our neighbors and our models, and the
day when it will be granted to us to imitate their example, we
would show that we have not degenerated from it" . . . But
the commissioning body understood nothing of the desires
I expressed. They thought I was mad. . . . Statues without
a pedestal! Where had that ever been seen before? There
must be a pedestal; there was no way of getting around it.[5]

As Carl Wendell Hines Jr. observed in his poem about Dr.
Martin Luther King Jr., after King's assassination, "Dead men
make such convenient heroes. . . . It is easier to build monuments
than to make a better world."[6]

"The Little Ones *Could* Be Saved"

We have the choice to be the Valley of Vision that stays clear and
close to God's intentions for us or that lets tumult, trampling,
and confusion reign. Our children's lives depend on the choice
we make.

It reminds me of an experience that Dutch feminist theologian
Johanna van Wijk-Bos recounted from her childhood. She was
born at the beginning of the Nazi occupation of the Netherlands
in 1940. She wrote,

In my village there lived a Jewish family named Frank [not
the family of Anne Frank] that had been part of the village
community for a long time. . . . At a certain point, it became
clear that this family had to go into hiding elsewhere. They
had two children, both girls, one only a baby. In making
their arrangements, the parents decided to take the older
child with them but leave the baby with a family in our

village for the duration of their time in hiding; it would be difficult to control a baby in a hiding place. Perhaps this decision was made for them. Who knows?

No sooner had the Franks gone than the woman who had agreed to take care of the baby reported the baby's presence to the mayor's office. The mayor was a well-known collaborator with the Nazis, and the baby girl disappeared into one of the death camps.[7]

Wijk-Bos wondered what changed the woman's mind, her resolve. Was it fear? Was it naïve conviction that no one would hurt a baby? Did the other horrified neighbors wish they were the ones who had agreed to protect the baby? She never knew, but it planted in her a deep outrage at injustice and horror at the abuse of power. "The littlest ones had their protection taken away from them and were delivered to the oppressor."[8] For that baby, that child, the village was not unlike the trampling, tumult, and confusion that held sway in the Valley of Vision so long ago.

Many years later, Wijk-Bos—now an adult—was in New York for a conference and got in a cab with colleagues. She wound up in the front seat next to the driver. She noticed his name on his driver's tag seemed Dutch, so she asked him about it. And here's what she wrote of their conversation:

"Yes," he said, "I am Dutch and I am Jewish. I emigrated shortly after the war."

Immediately I thought, How did you survive? He must have sensed my question.

"I was a youngster during the war, and people hid me in the village of Z. There were a lot of us there. Everybody knew the Jewish children, but we all survived because no one would tell the Germans who we were. The Germans were suspicious, of course. They even took one of the leaders of the Underground who helped to hide children and provide them with papers. They tortured him. He would not tell.

They continued to torture him, and he still would not tell. They finally killed him. Of this man I have a photograph in my house that will go to my children after I die. The picture has a place of honor in my house, and I have made my children swear to honor it after I am gone."[9]

There were a lot of us there. . . . We all survived. . . . The taxi driver's words reverberated in Wijk-Bos's mind and heart. "I sat awestruck. The village he had mentioned was only seven miles or so from the village where I had lived. It was possible, then; it had happened against the odds: the little ones *could* be saved."[10] That was a village, a valley, whose vision was not confused, whose vision was God's own vision where none would hurt or kill on God's holy mountain. A fourth-century desert father, Abba Antony, said, "Fear not this goodness as a thing impossible nor the pursuit of it as something alien, set a great way off; it hangs on our own choice."[11]

It is time for us—with courage, conviction, and caring; with persistence, passion, and urgency; and with vision and vigilance—to declare that our children can be saved from the more powerful forces that would surrender them as if it were necessity. We can become for our children the village of Z that says we won't abandon the children; we will protect them; we will save them from poverty, incarceration, and hunger, from abuse, neglect, and failing schools. We can end the unnecessary sacrifice of children on altars of adult's making and refuse to let tumult, trampling, and confusion reign. Let us become again a true and clear Valley of Vision for the sake of our children. May it be so. Amen.

～

Questions for Faithful Response

1. During the time of tumult and confusion in the Valley of Vision, the leadership headed for the hills. They scrambled for weapons, tore down homes to fill the breaches, and turned to distraction. How do you find that our nation

has responded during times of crisis or calamity? In what ways has it brought out our best values? In what ways has it revealed our abandoning them in the crisis?

2. What do you think it is in us that longs to place others on a pedestal as heroic leaders? What changes when we see those who have taken heroic actions as vulnerable and human?

3. The fourth-century desert father Abba Antony said, "Fear not this goodness as a thing impossible nor the pursuit of it as something alien, set a great way off; it hangs on our own choice." What helps you make the best choices for children? What gets in the way of your making choices that reflect God's intentions?

4. *Especially for parents and other caregivers:* Invite your child to draw a picture that shows how he or she thinks God wants our world to be—how people would treat one another—and then to tell you about it. Draw your own picture to share with your child, or make up a "choose your own adventure" story that offers your child choices to make along the way for what the main character should do in values-oriented situations. Then have your child make up a story so that you can make the choices. Talk together about real times that each of you has had to make a choice to help someone else, even when it was hard.

Part III

Sustained

Chapter Nine

Parables of Persistence

Luke 18

Then Jesus told them a parable about their need to pray always and not to lose heart. He said, "In a certain city there was a judge who neither feared God nor had respect for people. In that city there was a widow who kept coming to him and saying, 'Grant me justice against my opponent.' For a while he refused; but later he said to himself, 'Though I have no fear of God and no respect for anyone, yet because this widow keeps bothering me, I will grant her justice, so that she may not wear me out by continually coming.'" And the Lord said, "Listen to what the unjust judge says. And will not God grant justice to [God's] chosen ones who cry to [God] day and night? Will [God] delay long in helping them? I tell you, [God] will quickly grant justice to them. And yet, when the Son of Man comes, will he find faith on earth?"

(Luke 18:1–8)

The Parable 2000 Years Ago

Parables, like this one, are so rich with memorable characters that we are tempted to jump right to those archetypes. Parables are so encapsulated that it is easy to pop them out of the surrounding text and forget their place in the broader story. This parable is so familiar to us that we don't have to open a Bible to recite it.

But I have to confess, as familiar as this parable is, when I read it recently I realized that I couldn't precisely remember the context. Where was Jesus in his ministry when he told this? More important, what was going on for his *disciples* that this was the word Jesus knew they needed to hear?

It turns out they had been on the road awhile, journeying toward those defining final days in Jerusalem. It must have seemed a lifetime ago that the brothers dropped their nets to follow this one so eagerly. The teaching and healing in Capernaum the disciples witnessed must have seemed long past. Surely those demonstrations of God's power through Jesus to calm storms, still demons, end sickness, and restore children to life had made it seem to the disciples like it would always go easily. Those were heady days, days where victory seemed in hand, the reign of God so near.

And then . . . since Jesus, with his followers, turned his face to Jerusalem, it had seemed a harder, more daunting, wearying slog. In Samaria they faced rejection—we've been there, haven't we? There was the disappointing failure of three would-be followers—we've felt let down by the half-hearted commitment of others, haven't we? There was a point when even sisters were fighting among themselves as one felt like she was doing all the work—anyone else been there? There were warnings about the need to be watchful as they grew discouraged and distracted. There was lament over the city that kills the prophets. They faced growing political opposition, more rigid rejection from established religious authorities. Sound familiar?

It must have seemed like ages since Jesus had inaugurated his ministry by reading of good news to the poor and release to the captive and by announcing that Scripture had been fulfilled in their hearing. Surely his disciples wondered, at least on occasion, "If the good news in Scripture had been fulfilled back in Nazareth, why was ushering in that reign taking so long?"

This isn't a parable for those just starting out—for those fresh, heady days of new ministry when confidence abounds and expectations are high. This isn't a parable for followers who are finding the road easy, the job a cinch, and the crowds congenial. This isn't even a parable for those at the end of the journey. They don't need to hear this parable: we do. This is a parable for the weary when the road is long.

We need to hear again (and again and again) that powerful persistence and prayer can make the unjust back down. We need to hear again that God hears our prayers and will grant justice to us who cry to God night and day. We need to know afresh the enduring truth of Jesus' parable: what was true two thousand years ago was true two hundred years ago and twenty years ago, and it is true just as surely today.

Jesus not only offered this parable to those weary but willing followers, who never dreamed the journey would be so long— those discouraged and daunted disciples who hadn't known it would be so hard and who didn't know what or when the end of the journey would be reached: Jesus offered this parable even to us. "*In a certain city there was a judge who neither feared God nor had respect for people. In that city there was a widow who kept coming to him and saying, 'Grant me justice against my opponent. . . .'*"

The Parable Two Hundred Years Ago

We heard the parable as it transpired two thousand years ago. Here is the introduction to another parable as it was lived two hundred years ago.

> In a certain city named New Paltz there was a slave master who neither feared God nor had respect for people. And in that city, there was a woman called Isabella who kept coming and demanding justice for herself and her child.[1]

Isabella had escaped to freedom, a freedom subsequently made permanent when someone paid her former master for the balance of a year—long past the time when her former master had promised her freedom. Not long before her flight, however, the slave master had sold her child, a boy only five years old, to someone who took him to New York City on his way to England. But "finding the boy too small for his service," that man then sold Isabella's child to Solomon Gedney, who in turn sold the boy to a wealthy planter who took the child to Alabama. This was not only reprehensible, of course, but in fact illegal at the time: "The law expressly prohibited the sale of any slave out of the State, and all minors were to be free at twenty-one years of age." When the child was first sold, it was understood that he would be emancipated in New York.

Here is how Isabella described it to her friend Olive, who recorded it, what happened next: "When Isabel heard that her son had been sold South, she immediately started on foot and alone, to find the man who had thus dared, in the face of all law, human and divine, to sell her child out of the State; and if possible, to bring him to account for the deed." Arriving at New Paltz, she went directly to her former mistress, who dismissed Isabella's charges in the most insulting terms.

> Isabella heard her through, and after a moment's hesitation, answered in tones of deep determination—"*I'll have my child again.*"
> "Have *your child* again!" repeated her mistress—her tones big with contempt, and scorning the absurd idea of her getting him. "How can you get him? And what have you to support him with, if you could? Have you any money?"
> "No," answered Bell, "I have no money, but God has enough, or what's better! And I'll have my child again.". . . Speaking of it later, she said, "Oh my God! I know'd I'd have him agin. I was sure God would help me to get him. Why, I felt so *tall within*—I felt as if the *power of a nation* was with me!"

After finding her former mistress as heartless as the parable's judge, she went to Solomon Gedney's own mother and found her heartless as well—she compared the loss of Isabella's son to her own daughter's departure for marriage, with derisive laughter. "At this point, Isabella earnestly begged of God that he would show to those about her that He was her helper; and she adds, in narrating, 'And He *did;* or, if He did not show them, he did me.'"

At last, someone took her plight to heart and directed her to a sympathetic Quaker couple, who welcomed her into their home and then directed her to the courthouse, where she could enter a complaint to the Grand Jury in Kingston, New York. As she went to lodge her complaint, she encountered much difficulty and derision, but she persisted. At the courthouse, she was told to swear by the Bible that the child was her son. Unfamiliar with the ritual, she started to put the Bible to her lips to literally swear upon it, before the lawyer—amidst "uproarious laughter"— stopped her and had her rest a hand upon it. Finally, with a writ in hand to serve Solomon Gedney, she ran some *eight miles* to the constable. But the constable served the wrong man, which gave Gedney time to board a boat and evade accountability. It was nearly a year later that he finally returned with the child whom he had retrieved from the planter to whom he had sold him, yet he resumed his claim on the child as his property.

It had ever been Isabella's prayer, not only that her son might be returned, but that he should be delivered from bondage, and into her own hands, lest he should be punished out of mere spite to her, who was so greatly annoying and irritating to her oppressors; and if her suit was gained, her very triumph would add vastly to their irritation.

But the lawyer told her that her case had to wait until the next session of the court some months away. "The law must take its course," he said.

"What! wait another court! wait *months?*" said the persevering mother. "Why, long before that time, he can go clear off, and take my child with him—no one knows where. I *cannot* wait; I *must* have him *now*, whilst he is to be had."

The lawyer suggested that waiting shouldn't be a problem as Isabella would receive payment from the fine that would be levied against Gedney; but of course it wasn't money but her son that Isabella wanted.

> The lawyer used his every argument to convince her that she ought to be very thankful for what they had done for her; that it was a great deal, and it was but reasonable that she should now wait patiently the time of the court.
>
> Yet she never felt, for a moment, like being influenced by these suggestions. She felt confident she was to receive a full and literal answer to her prayer, the burden of which had been—"O Lord, give my son into my hands, and that speedily! Let not the spoilers have him any longer."
>
> Notwithstanding, she very distinctly saw that those who had thus far helped her on so kindly were wearied of her, and she feared God was wearied also."

How you wish there were someone then to have shared with her this parable and its promise that God never wearies of our prayers for justice!

And so she turned to Jesus, trusting in him as a sympathetic intercessor for the God she feared wearied of her prayers. And as she walked, despairing, a stranger asked her how it went getting her child back. She answered that everyone was tired of her and she had no one to help her. The stranger told her about a lawyer who could help, saying,

> "Lay your case before him; I think he'll help you. *Stick to him. Don't give him peace till he does. I feel sure if you press him, he'll do it for you.*"

She ran immediately to the lawyer who told her if she paid him five dollars he would get her son for her in twenty-four hours. She ran (without shoes) ten miles to a town where sympathetic Quakers donated the required sum, and then she ran the ten miles back.

> The lawyer now renewed his promise, that she should have her son in twenty-four hours. But Isabella, having no idea of this space of time, went several times in a day, to ascertain

if her son had come. Once, when the servant opened the door and saw her, she said, [with much surprise] "Why, this woman's come again!" [Isabella] then wondered if she went too often. When the lawyer appeared, he told her the twenty-four hours would not expire till the next morning; if she would call *then*, she would see her son. The next morning saw Isabella at the lawyer's door, while he was yet in his bed. He now assured her it was morning till noon; and that before noon her son would be there."

Finally, finally, the child, the mother, Solomon Gedney, the lawyer, and the judge gathered in the courtroom. When the pleading was at an end, the judge declared as a sentence of the court that Isabella's child be returned to her. Looking back on the experience, Isabella recalled:

"While, in deep affliction . . . labor[ing] for the recovery of her son, she prayed with constancy and fervor . . . 'Oh, God, you know how much I am distressed, for I have told you again and again. Now, God, help me get my son. If you were in trouble, as I am, and I could help you, as you can me, think I wouldn't do it? Yes, God, you *know* I would do it. . . . Oh, God, you know I have no money, but you can make the people do for me, and you must make the people do for me. I will never give you peace till you do, God. . . . Oh, God, make the people hear me—don't let them turn me off, without hearing and helping me."

She has not a particle of doubt that God heard her and especially disposed the hearts of thoughtless clerks, eminent lawyers, and grave judges and others—between whom and herself there seemed to her almost an infinite remove—to listen to her suit with patient and respectful attention, backing it up with all needed aid.

The sense of her nothingness in the eyes of those with whom she contended for her rights sometimes fell on her like a heavy weight, which nothing but her unwavering confidence in an arm which she believed to be stronger than all others combined could have raised from her sinking spirit.

"Oh! how little did I feel," [Isabella] repeated, ". . . . Oh, God only could have made such people hear me; and he did it in answer to my prayers."

Isabella—who came to be known as Sojourner Truth—was a living parable of persistence. Part of Isabella/Sojourner Truth's parable reminds us of the tension between the promise that justice will come quickly and the reality of injustice that seems to stretch on for an eternity. What do we do when "quickly" doesn't come fast? Every one of us can feel Isabella's agony with every day that passed without her son, her impatience with every one of those twenty-four hours the lawyer took.

In Luke's parable, we realize that the promise that God will quickly grant justice doesn't refer to time on the clock but to God's desire for justice, which precedes, accompanies, and lasts long beyond our prayers. It is the assurance that we don't have to convince God, like the judge, to desire justice, to grant justice— God already does. We misunderstand if we hear it as a promise of speed according to our sense of time rather than a promise about the nature of God: we don't have to convince God to be on the side of justice because that is where God has always been and always will be.

Still . . . when we know that children only get one childhood, one babyhood for brain development, one kindergarten year for reading readiness, one high school for college and career skills, it can be torturous to see years go by without the investments children need, without the policies and priorities that would protect those precious opportunities. When we hear that each Monday morning in some schools children race to the breakfast with extra urgency to finally fill small bellies that have been hungry since the school bell rang at the end of the previous Friday, we pray for justice to come *fast*.

And within the reality of justice that doesn't come as fast as we hope, we can find strength and inspiration in Isabella/Sojourner Truth: she literally ran a marathon—barefoot no less, back and forth between the funders and the lawyer, the Quakers and the court—to get her child returned. She ran with persistence, with a mother's love that never lets go, and with faith in God. And you and I can do no less in our marathon efforts to win justice for children. A sprint won't do it—we've got to be in this for the long run.

The Parable Twenty Years Ago

In a certain city, Mexico City, lived officials of a corrupt justice system that practiced torture and other human rights violations. In that same city there was a nun, Digna Ochoa, who was also a human rights attorney. Digna worked for a group called Centro Pro. It was dangerous work, as many of her clients had been victims of torture and other due-process violations at the hands of Mexican officials. As a result of her advocacy for these vulnerable clients, Digna herself became a target. She endured death threats, kidnapping, and a terrifying physical attack in which two men entered her apartment, bound and blindfolded her, interrogated her, and forced her to sign a statement before severing her phone lines and turning on the gas in her apartment, meaning to kill her. Digna survived and, undeterred, continued her courageous, persistent advocacy and efforts to reform the corrupt Mexican justice system.

A few weeks after the attack in her apartment, Digna spoke to the source of her persistence in the face of injustice and threats from the powerful, including death threats. She had shown a recently received death threat to another nun, Luz, who responded,

> "Digna, this is not a death threat. This is a threat of resurrection." That gave me great sustenance. . . .
>
> Now, some people said to me that my reaction was courageous. But I've always felt anger at the suffering of others. For me, anger is energy, it's a force. You channel energy positively or negatively. Being sensitive to situations of injustice and the necessity of confronting difficult situations like those we see every day, we have to get angry to provoke

energy and react. If an act of injustice doesn't provoke anger in me, it could be seen as indifference, passivity. It's injustice that motivates us to do something, to take risks, knowing that if we don't, things will remain the same. Anger has made us confront police and soldiers. . . . When they run into a woman, otherwise insignificant to them, who demands things of them and shouts at them in an authoritarian way, they are paralyzed. And we get results. I consider myself an aggressive person, and it has been difficult for me to manage that within the context of my religious education. But it does disarm authorities. . . . I give a certain mild image, but then I can, more efficiently, demand things, shout.[2]

Digna described one experience defending a man who had been missing for weeks, held in a military hospital despite the authorities' denials. Digna learned which state hospital he was being held in and went the next day to try to speak to him. She was denied access. Not one to give up, Digna reported,

I spent the whole morning studying the comings and goings at the hospital to see how I could get in. During a change in shifts, I slipped by the guards. When I got to the room where this person was, the nurse at the door told me I could not go in. "We are not even allowed in," she said. I told her that I would take care of myself; all I asked of her was that she take note of what I was going to do and that if they did something to me, she should call a certain number. I gave her my card. I took a deep breath, opened the door violently and yelled at the federal judicial police officers inside. I told them they had to leave, immediately, because I was the person's lawyer and needed to speak with him. They didn't know how to react, so they left. I had two minutes, but it was enough to explain who I was, that I had been in touch with his wife, and to get him to sign a paper proving he was in the hospital. He signed. By then the police came back, with the fierceness that usually characterizes their behavior. Their first reaction was to try to grab me. They didn't expect me to assume an attack position—the only karate position I know, from movies, I suppose. Of course, I don't *really* know karate, but they definitely thought I was going to attack. Trembling inside, I said sternly that if they laid a hand on me they'd see what would happen. And they drew back, saying, "You're threatening us." And I replied, "Take it any way you want."[3]

Digna drew strength from her faith and her religious community to manage her fear. Studying the Bible and other religious texts and group prayer helped during times of great danger, she shared, as well as her identity as a follower of Christ crucified for "denouncing the injustices of his time."[4]

Digna was assassinated in 2002. Her name means "worthy"; she is certainly worthy of sharing the mantle with the widow and Sojourner as an example of persistence in the face of injustice from the powerful. And I do believe that when her killers made good on the death threats, for Digna it was not a threat but a promise of resurrection.

In the parable in Luke, the judge's phrase "wear me out" literally means "give me a black eye." The judge feared that the widow, like a boxer, might give him a black eye. Digna spoke to the place of righteous anger—not hatred but *anger*. How do we harness our anger at injustice, our anger at zero-tolerance-discipline policies, our anger at racial profiling, at mass incarceration, at the whole cradle-to-prison pipeline? How can our outrage fuel our effectiveness?

Our Parables Today

We've heard the parable of two thousand years ago, two hundred years ago, and twenty years ago. How will it be told in our day of our lives? Who or what stands in for the unjust judge today? How will you run the marathon until justice is won? How will you harness your righteous anger? How will you look for someone who is weary on the way—someone wondering how long the road will be, why it is so hard—and how will you share with them the hope of the parable, the push to persist?

We can make a difference for children—our own children, children in our communities, and our nation's children—not only through caring encounters but also through public-policy changes that level the playing field and leave no child behind. Like Sojourner, will we act with a sense of urgency that refuses to be placated, that recognizes that every passing hour, day, and year that our children are not safe, supported, learning, and growing is too long to wait? When members of Congress, like Sojourner Truth's lawyer, try to placate us and counsel that we might need to wait for another session of Congress, will we insist like Sojourner that we cannot, *will not*, wait that long? When their schedulers express surprise that we are back to meet with them again, will we brush it off and insist on having our say? Will we, in effect, be on Congress's doorstep while they are still in their pajamas?

When we hit roadblocks—callous congresspeople, bogus budget arguments, tyrannical Tea Partiers—will we channel our anger and use it as a positive energy to overcome any and all we need to? Like Digna, will we rely on one another, on prayer, and on Scripture to gird ourselves for battle, to overcome fear?

Right now, we have the opportunity to see that our children have the experience of a CDF Freedom School program. At Freedom Schools, they sing a song titled "Something Inside So Strong." Like Sojourner Truth, children in CDF's Freedom School programs experience feeling "tall inside, like the power of a nation is in them." Every child should have a lasting experience like that—and we can make it happen.

Who else stands in, in your life, for the unjust judge? What situations call for your persistence, like the widow? I wonder, who do you—like Jesus—encounter that needs to hear this word, the parable of persistence, this assurance that God is, has always been, and will always be on the side of justice?

This parable is for them and for us as we pause thus far on the way. We're not just setting out, and we're not done yet. We have been treading a stony road with weary feet and will by God's might and grace keep in the path. We will persist and pray and work for justice because we love and serve a God who has been, is, and always will be on the side of justice. May it be so. Thanks be to God. Amen.

～

Questions for Faithful Response

1. We've heard the parable of persistence two thousand years ago, two hundred years ago, and twenty years ago. How will it be told in our day? What is your parable of persistence? Who or what stands in for the unjust judge today, for you?

2. What fuels your sense of urgency for action and change? Do you find yourself acting on that sense of urgency or quelling it? Why and how?

3. How do you understand the difference between destructive anger and righteous anger? How will you harness your righteous anger?

4. Digna, who experienced righteous anger, relied on colleagues, prayer, and Scripture to gird herself for battle and overcome fear. How are you or could you be connected to those sources of support in your life? What else helps you prepare for struggle and overcome fear so that you can act courageously for what is right?

5. Who do you know who is weary on the way, wondering how long the road will be and why it is so hard? How might you share with them the hope of the parable, the push to persist? Who do you know who needs to hear this word, the parable of persistence, this assurance that God is, has always been, and will always be on the side of justice?

6. *Especially for parents and other caregivers:* Talk with your children about a time that they wanted to give up when they were trying to do something that was hard. How did they feel when it wasn't working? What helped

them keep at it? If they did give up, what could have helped them to keep at it? Talk together about a big problem, something that is unfair, that they would want to change. Will it get solved quickly? What could keep you going to keep working to make it fair? Does God want us to work to solve problems and make things fair? How can praying help?

Chapter Ten

Vigilance

Hebrews 10

But recall those earlier days when, after you had been enlightened, you endured a hard struggle with sufferings, sometimes being publicly exposed to abuse and persecution, and sometimes being partners with those so treated. For you had compassion for those who were in prison, and you cheerfully accepted the plundering of your possessions, knowing that you yourselves possessed something better and more lasting. Do not, therefore, abandon that confidence of yours; it brings a great reward. For you need endurance, so that when you have done the will of God, you may receive what was promised. For yet,
"in a very little while,
the one who is coming will come and will not delay;
but my righteous one will live by faith.
My soul takes no pleasure in anyone who shrinks back."
But we are not among those who shrink back and so are lost, but among those who have faith and so are saved.

(Heb. 10:32–39)

Perhaps these words of Scripture were whispered into Harriet Tubman's ear by the Spirit in 1849 before she made her way from Maryland to freedom in Philadelphia. *"Recall those earlier days when . . . you endured a hard struggle with sufferings. . . . Do not, therefore, abandon that confidence of yours; it brings a great reward. For you need endurance."* Perhaps she recalled her sufferings in slavery or thought of how she had stood up for and literally put herself between an enraged overseer and the field hand who was the target of his anger, absorbing the blow of a heavy iron on the other's behalf. She did not shrink back then, and she did not shrink back once she decided to escape to freedom. She had a sure sense of the reliability of God's promise. When she reached the North for the first time, she later said, "There was such a glory over everything, the sun came like gold through the trees, and I felt like I was in heaven."[1]

"We are not among those who shrink back and so are lost, but among those who have faith and so are saved" (Heb. 10:39). Perhaps these were words that Harriet Tubman whispered to the others on her nineteen trips back to pick up passengers. "Do not abandon that confidence of yours; it brings a great reward. For you need endurance" (vv. 35–36). Perhaps she whispered those words to her sister and her sister's two young children as their small legs tired. Perhaps on a later, especially difficult trip, she whispered those words to her aged parents in their seventies.

Confidence, endurance, refusal to shrink back, sustaining faith: Harriet Tubman supremely embodied those qualities from this passage in Hebrews. Historians have written admiringly of her bold strategies to make her forays successful. She commandeered her master's horse and buggy at the beginning of her journey to freedom. She made the daring and difficult decision to turn south to evade slave hunters before resuming the northward journey. She fooled men reading a poster about her that described her as illiterate by pretending to read a book. John Brown called her "General Tubman" and described her as "one of the bravest persons on this continent." Frederick Douglass said, "Excepting John Brown—of sacred memory—I know of no one who has willingly encountered more perils and hardships to serve our enslaved people than [Harriet Tubman]."[2]

"We are not among those who shrink back and so are lost." Harriet Tubman once noted with justifiable pride that she "never lost a single passenger."[3]

The source of Harriet Tubman's confidence and endurance, her determination never to shrink back, was "her faith in God as deliverer and protector of the weak." "'I always tole God,' she said, 'I'm gwine [going] to hole stiddy on you, an' you've got to see me through.'"[4] Notes *Christianity Today*, "Tubman said she would listen carefully to the voice of God as she led slaves north, and she would only go where she felt God was leading her." Fellow abolitionist Thomas Garrett said of her that he had never met anyone who had more confidence in the voice of God.[5]

"Do not, therefore, abandon that confidence of yours; it brings a great reward. For you need endurance, so that when you have done the will of God, you may receive what was promised. . . . But we are not among those who shrink back and so are lost, but among those who have faith and so are saved."

Harriet Tubman was one in a succession of extraordinary, faithful women who did not abandon their confidence and received a great reward. Ida Wells-Barnett surely embodied that confidence as well. She stood up to a train conductor who sought to move her from her rightfully held first-class passenger seat in the ladies car to the Jim Crow car in 1884, and later she recalled,

I refused, saying that the forward car [closest to the locomotive] was a smoker, and as I was in the ladies' car, I proposed to stay . . . [The conductor] tried to drag me out of the seat, but the moment he caught hold of my arm I fastened my teeth in the back of his hand. I had braced my feet against the seat in front and was holding to the back, and as he had already been badly bitten he didn't try it again by himself. He went forward and got the baggageman and another man to help him and of course they succeeded in dragging me out.[6]

As she was dragged out amid the cheers and jeers of watching white men and women, did she have to whisper to herself,

"Do not abandon that confidence of yours, for it brings a great reward"? For she surely didn't abandon her confidence: when she returned to Memphis she hired an attorney to sue the railroad, winning in local circuit courts before her victory was overturned on appeal by the Supreme Court of Tennessee.

Her confidence and her recollection of her own hard sufferings surely fueled Mrs. Wells-Barnett's lifelong work for justice. She didn't shrink back from writing truth-telling editorials about the deplorable state of the schools, even though it resulted in her being fired from teaching. More than anything, her confidence, endurance, faith, and refusal to shrink back were evident in her crusade against lynching after her friend Tom Moss and his two friends were lynched. In her enormously influential 1892 pamphlet, *The Southern Horrors: The Lynch Law in All Its Phases*, Ida Wells-Barnett had the confidence to call out any and all who were complicit in their silence or with their voices—from the pulpit to the politicians to the press to the people. Listen to her courage in telling it like it is—she did not shrink back:

> The appeal of Southern whites to Northern sympathy and sanction. . . . has had its effect. It has closed the heart, stifled the conscience, warped the judgment and hushed the voice of press and pulpit on the subject of lynch law throughout this "land of liberty." Men who stand high in the esteem of the public for Christian character, for moral and physical courage, for devotion to the principles of equal and exact justice to all, and for great sagacity, stand as cowards who fear to open their mouths before this great outrage. They do not see that by their tacit encouragement, their silent acquiescence, the black shadow of lawlessness in the form of lynch law is spreading its wings over the whole country.
>
> Men who, like Governor Tillman, start the ball of lynch law rolling for a certain crime, are powerless to stop it when drunken or criminal white toughs feel like hanging an Afro-American on any pretext.
>
> Even to the better class of Afro-Americans the crime of rape is so revolting they have too often taken the white

man's word and given lynch law neither the investigation nor condemnation it deserved.

They forget that a concession of the right to lynch a man for a certain crime, not only concedes the right to lynch any person for any crime, but (so frequently is the cry of rape now raised) it is in a fair way to stamp us a race of rapists and desperadoes. They have gone on hoping and believing that general education and financial strength would solve the difficulty, and are devoting their energies to the accumulation of both.

The mob spirit has grown. . . . It has left the out-of-the-way places where ignorance prevails, has thrown off the mask and with this new cry stalks in broad daylight in large cities, the centers of civilization, and is encouraged by the "leading citizens" and the press.[7]

Following the publication of this and other writing, she helped organize the National Association of Colored Women and, personal and ideological differences with W.E.B. Du Bois notwithstanding, helped found in 1909 the NAACP, continuing to fight for justice until her final days. She was never one to shrink back. *"Do not, therefore, abandon that confidence of yours; it brings a great reward. For you need endurance, so that when you have done the will of God, you may receive what was promised. . . . But we are not among those who shrink back and so are lost, but among those who have faith and so are saved."*

Called to Vigilance

The community addressed by the letter to the Hebrews, on the other hand, was having a crisis of confidence as they watched and waited for God's coming reign. In the face of sustained struggle, painful persecution, and interpersonal differences, the community was falling into disarray. Some had even stopped meeting together, imagining they could just go it alone. Others were tempted to give up the faith altogether. To them were these words of warning and encouragement offered: hold fast to your confidence, endure, and don't shrink back—be *vigilant* as you await God's coming reign of freedom, love, and peace. What would help them do that was looking back and looking forward: calling on their shared memories, their history of standing together even across different experiences, and looking ahead with watchful, hopeful anticipation for the promised coming of God's love and justice. They were urged to stand together and keep looking out for one another as they watched and worked and waited for God's promised justice. They were urged, one might say, to become a vigilance committee.

In the abolitionist movement in Harriet Tubman's day and in the anti-lynching crusade of Ida Wells-Barnett's day, courageous individuals were helped to endure by the support of vigilance committees. Mind you, these were not vigil*ante* but vigilant or vigilance committees.

During slavery, vigilance committees formed to provide what those escaping slavery and seeking freedom needed. Some members of vigilance committees had themselves suffered in and escaped slavery. Other members hadn't experienced it themselves but stood alongside as partners with those who had. The vigilant committee provided money or in-kind resources to meet immediate needs like food, clothing, shelter, and health care. They provided legal assistance or networking, making connections to others who could help. In some places, vigilance committees of abolitionists challenged local, state, and federal policies. Members of vigilance committees testified in court. They practiced civil disobedience. They didn't just address the immediate crisis but also longer-term needs; in addition to helping those who were enslaved evade capture, they helped them settle into new lives and secure homes, jobs, and more. From Philadelphia, where Harriet Tubman first knew freedom, to Boston to Detroit and places in between, vigilance committees played an essential role in the abolitionist movement. While the Underground Railroad necessarily had to be kept from public eye, in some places the vigilance committees could publicly denounce injustice, publicly rally support, raise funds, challenge laws, petition for change, sway public opinion, and provide practical aid. Together, they exhibited and helped others to have confidence, endurance, and a refusal to shrink back born of their faith. During the anti-lynching crusade and early days of the NAACP, vigilance committees again played a crucial role—helping those seeking justice to endure and not shrink back. In the May 1913 issue of *The Crisis*, W. E. B. DuBois penned an editorial titled "The Vigilance Committee: A Call to Arms." He wrote,

There is scarcely a community in the United States where a group of colored people live that has not its vigilance committee. Sometimes this committee is organized and has a name indicating its function. Sometimes it is organized for other purposes and becomes a vigilance committee on occasion. In other cases the committee has no regular organization or members; it springs into being on occasion but consists of approximately the same group of persons from year to year.

The work of these vigilance committees is to protect colored people in their several communities from aggression. The aggression takes the form of hostile laws and ordinances, curtailment of civil rights, new racial discriminations, overtax or over-severe enforcement of the law, curtailment of opportunities, etc. Sometimes this aggression is but the careless act of thoughtless folk and needs but a word in season to correct it. More often it is a part of that persistent underground campaign centering largely among white Americans of Southern birth which is determined so to entrench color caste in the United States as to make it impossible for any person of Negro blood to be more than a menial. *servant*

Against both sorts of racial aggression organized effort is necessary. Many thoughtful colored people have sought to avoid this; to act independently and to refuse to meet organization by organization. This in most cases has been found impossible. The blows of racial and color prejudice fall on all alike, rich and poor, educated and ignorant, and all must stand together and fight.

> The methods of these vigilance committees are various. The simplest action is the appointment of a committee of one or more to call on some official or person of influence; from this, action extends to letters and the press, pamphlets, legislative hearings, mass meetings, petitions, etc. . . . The time is now evidently at hand to fund and pool this nation-wide experience and to systematize this scattered local effort into steady, persistent, and unwavering pressure. As it is, unorganized local efforts lack experience and knowledge of similar action elsewhere. Henceforth we must act together and we must fight continuously.[8]

The community to which the letter to the Hebrews was addressed was urged to be, in effect, a vigilance committee—to stick together with confidence, endurance, not shrinking back but holding fast to their faith as they waited for and witnessed to God's coming reign of justice. Harriet Tubman and others were strengthened and supported by abolitionist vigilance committees. Ida Wells-Barnett and others came together as vigilance committees.

And it seems to me that we are called to be the twenty-first-century vigilance committee for our children. To succeed at that mission, that calling, we have to stand together, stick together, meet together, and encourage one another so that we do not abandon our confidence but rather endure and never shrink back. With faith, we can work for and anticipate God's coming justice for our children. We can do so because we follow with confidence the One who endured even the cross, never shrinking back, that we might know ourselves loved and forgiven children of God. Thanks be to God. Amen.

∼

Questions for Faithful Response

1. The original vigilance committees came together to work against aggression in "the form of hostile laws and

ordinances, curtailment of civil rights, new racial discriminations, overtax or over-severe enforcement of the law,
curtailment of opportunities, etc."[9] How have you experienced or observed those forms of racial aggression in our
day? How might a modern-day vigilance committee work
to protect our children of color from such aggression and
put an end to it?

2. W. E. B. DuBois wrote, "Sometimes this aggression is but
   the careless act of thoughtless folk and needs but a word
   in season to correct it. More often it is a part of that persistent underground campaign."[10] Have you perceived a
   difference between "careless, thoughtless" racism and persistent, systemic racism designed to entrench white privilege? What response is called for in each instance? How
   does each form of racism affect children?

3. *The Crisis* editorial by DuBois called for united, collective efforts to end racism because "the blows of racial and
   color prejudice fall on all alike, rich and poor, educated
   and ignorant, and all must stand together and fight."[11]
   What have been for you the most inspiring or effective
   efforts or movements to unite against racism and other
   injustice? What dynamics work against united efforts in
   our day? With whom could you team up in the spirit of
   collaboration?

4. The original vigilance committees used a variety of methods: meeting with members of Congress or other leaders, writing letters to Congress and the media, publishing
   pamphlets, circulating petitions, calling for legislative
   hearings, and holding mass meetings. Which of these
   actions have you taken against racism or other injustice?
   Which would you be prepared to take, with others, to end
   racism?

5. *Especially for parents and other caregivers:* Talk with
   children about confidence. When do they feel confident?
   What helps them feel confident? Talk, too, about what

it means to be vigilant—to be watchful, on the lookout. Could they team up with their friends to be on the lookout for other children who need their help or friendship? Could they promise to stand together and speak out if they hear other children saying something unkind or unfair? What grown-ups could they count on if they needed support?

Chapter Eleven

Shepherd for the Lost

Matthew 18

"Take care that you do not despise one of these little ones; for, I tell you, in heaven their angels continually see the face of my Father in heaven. What do you think? If a shepherd has a hundred sheep, and one of them has gone astray, does he not leave the ninety-nine on the mountains and go in search of the one that went astray? And if he finds it, truly I tell you, he rejoices over it more than over the ninety-nine that never went astray. So it is not the will of your Father in heaven that one of these little ones should be lost."

(Matt. 18:10–14)

It was the kind of headline that stops you in your tracks: "Stricken Blind, Solo Pilot Is Guided to Safety."[1] The article that followed reported an astounding sequence of events. The sixty-year-old solo pilot of a small plane flying thousands of feet up in the air radioed an air traffic control tower in England, panicked because he couldn't see the control panel of his airplane and thought he might be momentarily blinded by the sunlight's glare. Asked if he wanted to continue flying to his original destination, the pilot said yes, imagining that he soon would once again see the control panel and safely find his way home.

Before long, he realized he was in grave danger—he still couldn't see even as his plane hurtled on. What he didn't know was that he had just had a stroke while in the air and the pressure on his optic nerve had cut off virtually all of his sight. What he did know was that he still couldn't see his control panel or the runway and wanted to land but didn't know how.

The distant voice from the control tower tried to give instructions from afar—monitoring the pilot's flight as a blip on the radar. But no matter how carefully worded the instructions were, the far-off voice couldn't help. The nose of the plane dipped; the plane's altitude began to plummet; and the air traffic controller realized the pilot was in utter peril.

A Royal Air Force pilot in the skies elsewhere was sent to find the blinded pilot. Soon he found the plane and positioned his own plane just 150 feet off the wing of the blind pilot. There, in the flesh, so close to the blind pilot, he could guide him better than the air traffic controller issuing instructions from afar. The pilot that had been sent to him saw and understood exactly what the blind pilot was going through. There, at his side, he guided him for more than forty minutes. You can just imagine him saying, "A little more to the left. Now raise the nose. Turn a bit to the right; that's it. Now stay straight, just as you're going. I'm right here. I won't leave you. I can see right where you are, and I can guide you home safely. I'm right here."

They approached the landing strip, and the pilot was still flying blind—"I cannot see the runway." The steady voice of the Royal Air Force pilot reassured him—"I can see it, and I will guide you—you'll see it soon; you'll see it soon." Finally, just before the blind pilot's plane touched the runway, he shouted to the guiding pilot—"I've got it now. I can see it! I can see!"

The Royal Air Force pilot said afterward that the air force had trained him to find lost planes and help them get back on course and find their way home but that he had never expected to guide a blind pilot. They have a name in the Royal Air Force, he said, for what he does. The RAF calls it "shepherding." "We are not used to shepherding blind pilots, which is what makes this amazing," he said.

When it won't do to simply issue instructions from afar, when what is needed to bring the lost home, to help the blind see where to go, is a personal, in-the-flesh, embodied, incarnate presence, it is called shepherding. Amazing grace, indeed.

You can't read that story—even written in the no-nonsense, secular style of the *New York Times*—and not think of the Good Shepherd. When I read it, the passage that came to mind was Matthew 18:10–14:

> "Take care that you do not despise one of these little ones; for, I tell you, in heaven their angels continually see the face of my Father in heaven. What do you think? If a shepherd has a hundred sheep, and one of them has gone astray, does he not leave the ninety-nine on the mountains and go in search of the one that went astray? And if he finds it, truly I tell you, he rejoices over it more than over the ninety-nine that never went astray. So it is not the will of your Father in heaven that one of these little ones should be lost."

How Are the Children?

It is not the will of God that one of these little ones should be lost. "How are the children?" is an African expression that's become known in child advocacy circles. Maasai warriors reportedly greet one another by asking, "How are the children?" Even those without biological children are asked this question; the question isn't asking after the children of any particular warrior but about all the children of the community, for what the tribe knows is that only when we can answer truly "all the children are well" will we know that the community itself is well.

Some congregations, as part of their Children's Sabbath celebrations, have printed up buttons and bumper stickers asking, "And how are the children?" United Methodist Bishop Sally Dyck wears such a button on her coat. She was in the airport, headed off on a trip, and the woman at the airline counter sized up her button and answered curtly, "*My* children are doing just fine, thanks!" The bishop recounted, "I told her I was glad that her children were doing fine, but we all need to make sure that *all* children are doing 'just fine.'"[2]

And how are the children? It is a question not about the ninety-nine children who are doing "just fine" but about the one who is lost, who needs our help, our protection, our care, our special efforts and advocacy.

Jesus might have said, "What do you think? If we have one hundred children, and twenty of them are living in poverty, isn't our role to provide the care and protection and love that will bring them into the experience of safety and security the others know?"

Might not Jesus have also said, "What do you think? If we have one hundred black boys in third grade, and you know that thirty-three of them are at risk of incarceration in their lifetime, shouldn't we protect them from the dangers and threats and harm of the cradle-to-prison pipeline so that they can know the safety and security the others enjoy?"

Can you not also hear this question: "What do you think? If we have a hundred children, and six of them are in harm's way because they lack health care, shouldn't we do whatever it takes to bring them into the fold of health coverage?"

I tell you, it is not the will of God that even one of these little ones be lost. Even as we rejoice and give thanks for the well-being of those who thrive, we are expected to do whatever it takes to bring the others home to an experience of safety, security, plenty, and purpose.

Seeking the Lost, Learning from the Young

As with many of these things, sometimes children seem to get it better than adults of our nation and world. Waitaka was a little boy who knew what it means to go out looking for the one in danger, the one that is lost. Ingrid Monroe, who later became his adoptive mother, told me of her son's life before he came to her family. Waitaka was one of Nairobi's many street children, fending for himself on the hard and dangerous streets as best as a four-year-old, then five-year-old, then six-year-old could.

Then, when Waitaka was six, he was run over by a bus rumbling through the streets and was taken to a hospital, where they did what they could to save his legs. They were able to, barely; Waitaka was "crippled"—their word—but with pain and difficulty he could walk.

When he was ready to leave the hospital, he was taken by a Catholic priest, Father Grohl, to live in an orphanage, the Undugu Home, founded by the priest. For the first time in his life, Waitaka had a warm house to stay in, a soft bed to sleep on, food to eat, and adults to protect him.

But to the adults' bewilderment, and then frustration and even anger, Waitaka kept running away. When no one was watching, the little boy would hobble out the doors of the home, turning his back on the safety and shelter, and venture out into the dark and dangerous streets. Time and again they would bring him back, and then before they knew it, he would head out again, limping back into the streets.

Finally, the staff washed their hands of him—he's nuts, they said; he doesn't want to stay in the home. They gave up on him.

What the staff didn't know was that the reason Waitaka kept running away was because he was looking for his little brother Kareithi. He couldn't bear to stay, comfortably ensconced in the home, when his little brother was still out there, lost, hungry, scared, homeless.

One day Ingrid learned from Father Grohl that Waitaka had run away again and the staff was not going to go after him— they had given up on him. She said to Father Grohl, "If you can find him one more time, bring him to my home." They did, and Waitaka finally stayed, as Ingrid and her husband joined Waitaka in the search for Kareithi. Day after day, month after month, year after year they searched; and then after three years they finally found him. They discovered that Kareithi had been arrested when he was four years old. He had been in prison for almost four years before they found him and brought him into their family.

Waitaka, this one little boy determined to bring his lost brother into the fold, didn't stop, but he also couldn't do it alone—he needed the help of other committed shepherds, adults like Ingrid and Father Grohl, who also wouldn't give up looking.

Why don't we have that same relentless sense of purpose and mission that won't let us rest until we know that every child has what we ourselves enjoy? You have to wonder, how is it that a six-year-old boy can turn his back on comfort and security to go out into the dark and danger to find another, even more vulnerable child who is still lost—poor, hungry, and then imprisoned—and yet every day adults in our nation rest in their own comfort and security, their own warm homes with plentiful food, and don't do what they need to do to bring all children who know poverty, hunger, lack of health care, and imprisonment to a place of safety and security, to a national house that is warm and welcoming and provides what they need?

It is not the will of our God that even one of these little ones be lost. When will we do what it takes to follow in the footsteps of the Good Shepherd so that not one is given up for lost?

I Will Never Let You Go

Anne Hjelle is one who knows what it means not to be given up for lost. Anne is part of a loose-knit mountain-biking group called the Trail Angels.[3] Anne and her friend Debbi Nicholls were up in the mountains of California, biking on the dusty red dirt trails one day. Seemingly out of nowhere, in a blur of fur and fangs, a mountain lion leapt from the bushes and knocked Anne from her bike. He clamped his jaws on her helmeted head and began to drag her, screaming, into the bushes.[4]

Debbi, just a few yards behind, didn't hesitate. She jumped off her bike and threw it at the mountain lion. But that didn't scare it into releasing Anne, and the mountain lion continued to pull her into the bushes for the final kill.

Debbi didn't run away; she didn't stand at a distance; she didn't hesitate; she didn't seek to save her own life. Instead, she grabbed the leg of her friend and held on with all of her might. The mountain lion momentarily released its hold on Anne's head before biting her face and then continued trying to overpower

Debbi's hold and pull Anne away. Several other mountain bikers came upon them at this moment. One recalled the scene for a reporter: "Debbi was yelling at us. She was hanging on to Anne's legs, and the mountain lion had Anne's head, her face in its jaw, and it was a tug-of-war." The other bikers began to throw rocks at the mountain lion.

Part of her face torn off, her head in the lion's mouth, Anne moaned, "I'm going to die."[5] Debbi, still holding on to Anne's leg, scrabbling to get a foothold in the rocky dirt and fighting with all her might, replied with fierce determination, "You're not. I will never let you go."

Anne moaned, "Dear God, dear God," and lost consciousness.[6]

Debbi never stopped holding on until her love that would never let Anne go triumphed over the cruel ferocity of the mountain lion. The mountain lion turned tail and ran. Debbi pulled Anne a slight distance away and stayed with her until she was airlifted to Mission Hospital.

"I will never let you go," Debbi told Anne. *So it is not the will of your God in heaven that one of these little ones should be lost. I will never let you go.*

When I picture God as Shepherd now, it's not always a pastoral image of a shepherd standing and gazing watchfully over the sheep. Sometimes the image is of a limping six-year-old leaving the warm shelter of his home to look for his little brother in the cold and dangerous streets. Sometimes, now, my image of the Good Shepherd is of a woman scrabbling in the dirt on the dusty mountainside, holding on fiercely to the leg of a beloved one, fighting the might of a mountain lion with a mightier love that says, "I will never let you go."

And we who know that fierce love that never lets go from our Shepherd can do no less for our children, for all children. It is not the will of our God that even one of these little ones should be lost, and so when they are lost and left behind on the streets, homeless, or imprisoned, it is our job to keep going out after them even when it means leaving our comfort and security behind. It means that when they are in the jaws of poverty, violence, abuse, lack of health care, or failing schools, it is our job to grab onto their legs, and when they are ready to give up, it is our job to declare, "I will never let you go. *I will never let you go.*" And to win that struggle. We can do no less. May it be so. Amen.

~

Questions for Faithful Response

1. When it's not enough to issue instructions from afar, when what is needed to bring the lost home and help the blind see is a personal, in-the-flesh, embodied, incarnate presence, it is called shepherding. What does the incarnation of God in Jesus mean for you and your faith? How have you experienced God through the caring of others?

2. How would you respond to the Maasai greeting "How are the children?"

3. Who are the children or families that you think we, as a nation or congregations, have "given up for lost"? What would persisting with determination to assure that all children and families know safety look like in your life, congregation, or community?

4. Sometimes children seem to understand things better than adults. When have you learned something from a child or appreciated the moral clarity with which a child regarded and responded to a problem?

5. How do you understand the priorities of the biblical passage for our day and our concern for children? By ordinary accounting, there is great illogic in leaving the vast majority, who are safe, to go out after the few who have strayed into trouble to bring them to safety. The parable, however, invites us not to ordinary accounting but to "new math" that seeks out the few, the last, the lost, and the least. What could that mean for how we approach serving and advocating for children at greatest risk?

6. When you picture God as a good shepherd, what do you see? When have you been in the role of a good shepherd

for a child or children? Who else have you seen as such a shepherd?

7. ***Especially for parents and other caregivers:*** With young children, retell the Good Shepherd story—perhaps using stuffed animals to stand in for the "sheep." Invite the children to wonder aloud with you about why the shepherd went off in search of the lost one. What do they think this tells us about how God cares for every single one of us? Think together about ways that you can show that same caring love for children who are left out or don't have the safety and things they need.

Chapter Twelve

Godspeed

Deuteronomy 16

You shall appoint judges and officials throughout your tribes, in all your towns that the LORD your God is giving you, and they shall render just decisions for the people. You must not distort justice; you must not show partiality; and you must not accept bribes, for a bribe blinds the eyes of the wise and subverts the cause of those who are in the right. Justice, and only justice, you shall pursue, so that you may live and occupy the land that the LORD your God is giving you.

(Deut. 16:18–20)

Is This as Fast as It Goes?

It was a foggy day at Washington's Dulles airport. I boarded the plane bound for Florida to give a speech. On my sixth flight of the month, I settled myself into my seat and immediately buried myself in some work. As I did so, a father and his young son, maybe three years old, entered the row in front of me. On what was clearly his first-ever airplane ride, the little boy eagerly clambered into his window seat, pushed up the plastic shade, and peered out the window with great excitement and anticipation.

Well, the deep fog that day had delayed many flights. Our plane was way at the back of a long line of planes waiting for their turn on the runway. So you know what that means: the plane at the front of the line would take off, and then the rest of us in this long line of planes would roll slowly forward a few feet and then stop and wait some more. Then the next plane would take off, and we would inch forward, stop, wait, and so on. Buried in work, I scarcely paid attention as for half an hour or more we continued inching forward like this.

Suddenly I heard the little boy turn to his dad and ask with dismay and deep disappointment, "Is this as fast as it goes?"

I wonder if, given the opportunity, our nation's more than 14 million children who live in poverty, who are waiting for us to end child poverty in our rich nation, would turn to each of us and ask, "Is this as fast as it goes?" Is this as fast as we can end poverty while their childhoods slip by?

I wonder if the hungry children whose parents are waiting to hear if the SNAP program—food stamps—will be cut or preserved, whose meals depend on the appropriations decisions of Congress, would turn to our legislators and ask, "Is this as fast as it goes?" Is this as fast as we can go to protect children from cuts to programs they count on?

I wonder if the three-year-old waiting for a place in Head Start to be funded, or the toddler waiting for a quality child-care spot, or a child at the bottom of the list for affordable housing would ask us all, "Is this as fast as it goes?"

I wonder if the nation's uninsured children—who rely on Medicaid, jeopardized by budget cuts, on health reform, threatened with repeal—would turn to pundits and pastors, congregations and Congress, and ask, "Is this as fast as it goes?" Is this as fast as we can go to protect every child with health coverage?!

Is this as fast as we can go? No!

Pursuing Justice

Our passage from Deuteronomy warns against distorting justice and the things that can fog our leaders' clarity about the right thing to do, slowing our progress toward justice. Babies, now as then, aren't very good at making bribes; children don't make campaign contributions, or vote, or lobby, or do much of anything to tip the scales in their favor. Children and their cause are outweighed by contributors, campaigners, corporations, and constituents. It's an old, old story. Isaiah, using the same Hebrew word for *pursue* as this writer of Deuteronomy, says of the nation's leaders,

> Everyone loves a bribe
> and runs after [pursues] gifts.
> They do not defend the orphan,
> and the widow's cause does not come before them.
> (Isa. 1:23b)

Both writers warn of a nation headed fast in the wrong direction and of children and poor parents being left behind.

In our passage, we are not only warned of the dangers of distorting or subverting justice. We are told to *pursue* justice. There can be nothing accidental or incidental, apathetic or apolitical, about pursuing justice. Rabbi Abraham Heschel knew something about pursuing justice. He said once, after marching with Dr. King in Selma, "It felt as if my feet were praying." Of this passage in Deuteronomy, Rabbi Heschel wrote, "The term 'pursue' carries strong connotations of effort, eagerness. This implies more than merely respecting or following justice"; we must actively pursue it.[1]

The writer of Deuteronomy couldn't have envisioned, precisely, our burgeoning e-mail inboxes, phones that ring off the hook, computers waiting for us to finish memos or homework or grant reports. But maybe he knew, nonetheless, that there would always be competition between our to-do lists and the call to do justice, and if we are not to be forever distracted and derailed from doing justice by the rest of our over-full lives and competing demands, then we would have to pursue, actively *pursue*, justice with focus, urgency, energy, imagination, and determination.

Dr. King underscored the imperative of pursuing justice with speed and focus when he said in a speech at Riverside Church,

"We are now faced with the fact that tomorrow is today. We are confronted with the fierce urgency of now. In this unfolding conundrum of life and history there is such a thing as being too late. . . ." He concluded, "We must move past indecision to action."[2]

So how fast are we going to get to work? How fast are we going to tell our nation's leadership to get moving? How are we going to remind them that their first responsibility is to defend the orphan—that is, our nation's poorest and most vulnerable children—and to respond to the widow's cause—that is, the parents who are most impoverished, most lacking in community and economic supports? How much fierce urgency will we expect from one another and ourselves in the pursuit of justice at this crucial time?

Victor

Maybe you remember the story in the news some years ago of Victor Perez, an immigrant here legally, a construction worker by trade but unemployed for three years, picking grapes to try to make ends meet for his family. On this fall day he was standing outside his house in Fresno, California, talking with his cousin about a recent Amber Alert for an eight-year-old girl who had been abducted. As they were standing there talking, he spotted a vehicle that looked like the one in the Amber Alert.

So Victor leapt into his own car and took off in pursuit, even though he was nervous that the man driving the vehicle might have a weapon. Victor pulled up to try to cut off the vehicle and the man driving protested, "I don't have no time," and sped up to try to get away. Victor kept pursuing him.[3]

Victor later said, "The second time I reached him, the way he acted—yes, I was, for a split second I was nervous until I saw the little girl and all fear was out the window after that, I didn't have no fear. I wasn't thinking of me no more. I was just thinking we need to get that little girl to safety." He added, "I wasn't going to give up. . . . I couldn't give up."[4] So Victor kept pursuing him.

The abductor was pushing the little girl down as he drove, trying to hide her. Victor said, "He kept getting away. He kept going round my truck. The last time I completely said, 'Either he crashes into me or he stops.'"[5] Finally, on his fourth attempt, Victor forced the vehicle to stop, and the abductor shoved the child out. She was saved because Victor hadn't hesitated in his pursuit. Victor was, I think, aptly named.

Afterward, Victor humbly said, "I just felt like I was doing my part. . . . I just felt like everybody should step up in their own communities and when something like this happens, come together and try to do your part to help out. And, you know," Victor concluded, "I just thank God I was put in the right situation to do what I did."[6]

Amber Alert Time for Our Nation's Children

When a child is in absolute jeopardy and in mortal danger, we put out an Amber Alert—we tell the whole community that we are in pursuit of the child and the one who is endangering her or him. It is a time of utmost urgency, and everyone has to get involved. Everyone is expected to be aware, to look out for the child, and to do what he or she can to help rescue the child in danger.

This is Amber Alert time for our nation's children. Everyone in our communities of faith needs to be on the lookout for the child and needs to help in the pursuit in order to bring the child to safety and see that justice is done. We need to protect children from cuts, invest in their development, and see that the rich and powerful contribute their fair share.

In an Amber Alert, the child's face, name, and story are plastered on telephone poles, on TV and text alerts, and in the newspaper. In this Amber Alert time for our nation's children, we won't get to see the faces of all 14.5 million children in poverty, or the millions without needed health care, or those without a spot in Head Start or child care, or the countless faces of children who went to bed hungry last night. We won't come to know their names or faces as intimately as we do when an Amber Alert goes out for a single child. Perhaps, however, we can meet just a few, as described in the Children's Defense Fund "New Faces of Poverty" series:

> Shoes tell the story of the McKee family's descent into poverty. Those of Skyler, who is 10, and Zachery, who is 12, are falling apart—tops flapping loose above the worn remnants of soles from which they have largely detached. When their big sister, Jordan, 14, plays on her school's volleyball team, she wears the varsity coach's shoes.
>
> Less visible is hunger. The children and their parents, Tonya and Ed McKee, who live in Michigan, sometimes went without food this summer when Ed's unemployment insurance ran out and the family was not yet receiving food stamps. Skyler said he gave the birthday money he got at church to his mom for groceries "and I told her she didn't have to pay me back." Skyler confided that sometimes his stomach has growled. "It's hard not easy like it was before where we had money and could do stuff. Now we don't go anywhere. . . . Sometimes we don't have food and we just don't eat."
>
> Their mother Tonya shared, "Ed and I went hungry some nights so we could feed the kids. A lady here in town has brought us food several times and went shopping for us several times. And our parents helped when they could. Otherwise, we didn't know where the next meal would come from. One of my friends brought over some cereal and milk one day and the boys said, 'Wow! We get cereal!'"[7]

I can imagine that you, too, have children in difficult or desperate circumstances that you hold in your heart. Perhaps there is a child you met at your congregation's food pantry or clothes closet when he or she came with his or her family for food or to get a pair of shoes. The way that you know them—their names, stories, faces, or even this glimpse of the McKee children—that's more than we'll get of most of our nation's millions of children in peril. We'll never come to know all 14.5 million children personally, but *God* knows each of their names, their faces, their stories. And God calls us to go in pursuit of justice on their behalf.

Godspeed

Back in the Middle Ages, people used the expression "Godspeed"; it was shorthand for "God speed you." "Godspeed," they would say, meaning "May God send you swiftly on your way." It was a wish for success and a prosperous journey, a hope that you would quickly reach your desired destination or goal. "Godspeed."

We don't have time to move at the world's sluggish pace to rescue our children. We don't have time for filibustering in Congress and for frittering away our own time; we don't have time for business-as-usual foot dragging at the Capitol or slogging our way through our own routines. We can't keep moving at the world's pace if we are going to protect children as God expects of us. This *isn't* as fast as it goes. As we pursue justice as God intends, we need, my friends, to say to one another as a blessing, a reminder, and a prodding, "Godspeed."

Justice, only justice, shall you pursue. May it be so. Godspeed.

~

Questions for Faithful Response

1. Do you think our nation is moving as fast as it can to secure justice for children? What do you think is accelerating change, and what do you think is delaying it?

2. We will "always find ourselves in competition between our to-do lists and the call to do justice, and if we are not to be distracted from doing justice because of our busy lives, then we will need to pursue justice with focus, urgency, energy, imagination, and determination. What gets in the way of your work for justice?

3. In what ways should we tell our nation's leadership to get moving? How are we going to remind them that their first responsibility is to defend the orphan—that is, our

nation's poorest and most vulnerable children—and to respond to the widow's cause—that is, the parents who are most impoverished, most lacking in community and economic supports?

4. How did you feel when you read about the McKee family? What other personal stories of families in difficult circumstances have touched you? Who are the children in difficult or desperate circumstances that you hold in your heart?

5. What difference does it make in acting for children when we know them by name, face, and story? What can we do to generate that same sense of caring and urgency when we need to act for great numbers of children we don't know by name?

6. *Especially for parents and other caregivers:* Seek out good children's books that will help your child "meet" other children in difficult circumstances. (*Something Beautiful* by Sharon Dennis Wyeth is just one example.) Talk about what that child and her/his family and others who care could do to make things better. Then, talk about what your child and your family could do to make things better for children in similar circumstances—optimally working in partnership with the children and families and getting to know them personally. Talk with your children about the difference between making things better right away for one person (active caring) and making things fair and preventing problems for many people (working for justice). Both are important.

Resources for Faithful Child Advocacy from the Children's Defense Fund[1]

The Children's Defense Fund

The Children's Defense Fund Leave No Child Behind® mission is to ensure every child a Healthy Start, a Head Start, a Fair Start, a Safe Start, and a Moral Start in life and successful passage to adulthood with the help of caring families and communities. CDF provides a strong, effective, and independent voice for *all* the children of America who cannot vote, lobby, or speak for themselves. CDF pays particular attention to the needs of poor children, children of color, and those with disabilities. CDF educates the nation about the needs of children and encourages preventive investments before they get sick, drop out of school, get into trouble, or suffer family breakdown. CDF began in 1973 and is a private, nonprofit organization supported by individual donations and foundation, corporate, and government grants.

From its inception, CDF has worked in partnership with people of faith from across the religious spectrum. Religious people and organizations—with millions of members with deep roots in communities across the country, a history of caring for children, and moral authority—are indispensable to building a successful Leave No Child Behind® movement. With our collective voice, followed by concrete action, we do not just make small changes. We change the community. We change the nation. We

135

change the lives and improve the odds for all children. Learn more, find resources, and sign up for alerts and information at www.childrensdefense.org.

The National Observance of Children's Sabbaths

Each October, thousands of faith communities participate in the multifaith National Observance of Children's Sabbaths® weekend. Traditionally celebrated the third weekend of October, the Children's Sabbath brings together Christian, Jewish, Muslim, Bahá'í, Hindu, Sikh, Buddhist, and other communities, as well as multifaith coalitions that lift up children in need and answer their own faith tradition's call to pursue justice, mercy, and compassion for our most vulnerable. The National Observance of Children's Sabbaths is coordinated by the Children's Defense Fund in partnership with hundreds of endorsing denominations and religious organizations.

Each year CDF provides a multifaith Children's Sabbath resource manual to assist congregations and communities. The Children's Sabbath resource manual provides planning suggestions; worship resources, including prayers, sermon notes, and sample liturgies; education resources for all ages; action ideas for the Children's Sabbath weekend and throughout the year; and more. The Children's Sabbath resource manual is typically available for download, free of charge, from the Children's Defense Fund website: www.childrensdefense.org.

CDF's Samuel Dewitt Proctor Institute for Child Advocacy Ministry

CDF's Samuel DeWitt Proctor Institute for Child Advocacy Ministry provides spiritual renewal, continuing education, intergenerational movement-building workshops, and networking as Christians from across the denominational spectrum explore how their faith calls them into ministries of child advocacy and guides, shapes, and sustains them in their work with and for children.

The Proctor Institute is held Monday through Friday during the third week of July each year at CDF Haley Farm in Clinton, Tennessee. Join clergy, seminarians, Christian educators, young adult leaders, and other faith-based advocates for children to gain new inspiration, information, and ideas from preachers and noted plenary speakers who are making a difference to end child poverty and dismantle the Cradle to Prison Pipeline®. Come for an experience of Beloved Community, and join in the intergenerational, interracial, and multiethnic conversation with people who share your passion for justice for our nation's children. For more information or to register visit www.childrensdefense.org.

CDF Freedom Schools® Program

The CDF Freedom Schools® program seeks to build strong, literate, and empowered children prepared to make a difference in themselves, their families, communities, nation, and world today. By providing summer and after-school reading enrichment for children who might otherwise not have access to books, the CDF Freedom Schools program plays a much-needed role in helping to curb summer learning loss and close achievement gaps—and is a key part of CDF's work to ensure a level playing field for all children. In partnership with local congregations, schools, colleges and universities, community organizations, and secure juvenile justice facilities, the CDF Freedom Schools program boosts student motivation to read, generates more positive attitudes toward learning, increases self-esteem, and connects the needs of children and families to the resources of their communities. Since 1995, more than 137,000 preK–12 children have had a CDF Freedom Schools experience and more than 16,000 college students and young adult staff have been trained by CDF to deliver this empowering model.

The CDF Freedom Schools model incorporates the totality of the Children's Defense Fund's mission by fostering environments that support children and young adults to excel and believe in their ability to make a difference. Site coordinators and project directors are also trained by CDF to provide supervision and administrative oversight.

The program provides an exciting Integrated Reading Curriculum (IRC), including carefully chosen developmentally appropriate and culturally relevant books. The model curriculum supports children and families around five essential components.

See more at http://www.childrensdefense.org.

Notes

Chapter 1: From Weeping to Work

1. Sharon LaFraniere, "Africa's World of Forced Labor, in a 6-Year-Old's Eyes," *New York Times*, October 29, 2006, http://www.nytimes.com/2006/10/29/world/africa/29ghana.html?pagewanted=all&_r=1&.
2. "An African Tale to Break Your Heart (6 Letters)," *New York Times*, October 31, 2006, http://www.nytimes.com/2006/10/31/opinion/l31child.html.
3. The Children's Defense Fund, *The State of America's Children 2016* (Washington, DC: Children's Defense Fund, 2016). These and all following data are from *The State of America's Children 2016*, which made calculations based on the poverty data from 2015—the most recent available. Visit the Children's Defense Fund website at www.childrensdefense.org for additional information and data, which are updated annually or as new numbers become available.
4. Ibid, 6.
5. Children's Defense Fund, "Juvenile Justice," http://www.childrensdefense.org/policy/justice/, accessed January 12, 2016.
6. Linda Waldman, *My Neighborhood: The Words and Pictures of Inner-City Children* (Chicago: Hyde Park Bank Foundation, 1993), 24.
7. Kathleen M. O'Connor, "Jeremiah," in *The Women's Bible Commentary*, 3rd ed., ed. Carol A. Newsom and Sharon H. Ringe (Louisville, KY: Westminster John Knox Press, 2012), 276.
8. *The State of America's Children 2014*, 5.
9. Children's Defense Fund, "CDF Freedom Schools Program," http://www.childrensdefense.org/programs/freedomschools/.
10. Erik Tryggestad, "Oprah Winfrey Puts Ministry's 'Magnificent Seven' in Spotlight," *Christian Chronicle*, March 2007, http://www.christianchronicle.org/article/oprah-winfrey-puts-ministrys-magnificent-seven-in-spotlight.

11. Sharon LaFraniere, "Building a Memorial to a Son, One Child at a Time," *New York Times*, February 5, 2007, http://www.nytimes.com/2007/02/05/world/africa/05ghana.html?_r=0.
12. Tryggestad, "Oprah Winfrey."

Chapter 2: Sing a New Song

1. *Invictus*, directed by Clint Eastwood (Warner Brother Pictures, 2010), DVD.
2. Statistics marked with * are based on 180 school days a year. The Children's Defense Fund, *The State of America's Children 2016* (Washington, DC: Children's Defense Fund, 2016). These and all following data are from the *The State of America's Children 2016*, which made calculations based on the poverty data from 2015—the most recent available. Visit the Children's Defense Fund website at http://www.childrensdefense.org for additional information and data, which are updated annually or as new numbers become available.
3. J. Clinton McCann, "Psalms," in *The New Interpreter's Bible*, vol. 4, ed. Leander E. Keck et al. (Nashville: Abingdon Press, 1996), 809.
4. "Barbara Johns," Congress of Racial Equality, accessed December 9, 2013, http://www.core-online.org/History/barbara_johns1.htm (interview no longer available).
5. Ibid.
6. Ibid.
7. Juan Williams, *Eyes on the Prize* (New York: Penguin Books, 1988), 177.
8. Ibid.
9. Ibid.

Chapter 3: Stumbling Blocks and Cornerstones

1. Children's Defense Fund, *The State of America's Children 2016* (Washington, DC: Children's Defense Fund, 2016).
2. Gene M. Tucker, "The Book of Isaiah 1–39," in *The New Interpreter's Bible*, vol. 6, ed. Leander E. Keck et al. (Nashville: Abingdon Press, 2001), 239–40.
3. Ibid., 239.
4. Gary Bellow, "Speech before the Alliance for Justice" (speech, Alliance for Justice, Washington, DC, April 30, 1996).

Chapter 4: Troops, Trumpets, and Torches

1. Gene Sharp, *From Dictatorship to Democracy: A Conceptual Framework for Liberation*, 4th U.S. ed. (East Boston: Albert Einstein Institution, May 2010), 8.
2. CDF's Child Watch program is a guided site visitation program in which local organizers take community leaders to see, firsthand, sites that shed light on the problems facing children (such as a homeless shelter, neonatal intensive care unit, or juvenile detention facility) and then take them to sites that demonstrate solutions (such as transitional housing and job-training programs, community health clinics, and afterschool programs teaching

restorative justice practices). At the end of the visits, participants debrief to consider how they can work to prevent the problems and promote the solutions.

3. Mother Jones, *The Autobiography of Mother Jones*, ed. Mary Field Parton (Chicago: Charles H. Kerr & Co., 1925), http://digital.library.upenn.edu/women /jones/autobiography/autobiography.html. All subsequent quotes by Mother Jones were taken from this source.

Chapter 5: What's Next?

1. Vincent Harding, *Martin Luther King: The Inconvenient Hero* (Maryknoll, NY: Orbis Books, 2008), 72.
2. Martin Luther King, Jr., *The Trumpet of Conscience*, in *A Testament of Hope: The Essential Writings and Speeches of Martin Luther King, Jr.*, ed. James M. Washington (New York: HarperOne, 1986), 634.
3. Harding, *Martin Luther King*, 70.
4. Prathia Hall, "Freedom-Faith," in *Hands on the Freedom Plow: Personal Accounts by Women in SNCC*, ed. Faith S. Holsaert et al. (Chicago: University of Illinois Press, 2010), 173.
5. Ibid., 173–74.
6. Abraham Heschel, *The Prophets* (New York: HarperPerennial Modern Classics, 2001), 365.

Chapter 6: Team of Rivals

1. Graham Hayes, "Central Washington Offer the Ultimate Act of Sportsmanship," ESPN.com, April 28, 2008, http://sports.espn.go.com/ncaa /columns/story?id=3372631. Subsequent quotes from this story were taken from this online source.
2. The NCAA later clarified that this had been a misinterpretation of the rules and a substitution could have been made. However, during that particular game, both teams and officials were acting according to the misunderstanding that Sara's team could not help her.

Chapter 7: Certainly Not

1. Howard Zinn, "Mississippi: Hattiesburg," in *The Zinn Reader* (New York: Seven Stories Press, 2009), 96.
2. Nelson Mandela, *Long Walk to Freedom: The Autobiography of Nelson Mandela* (New York: Back Bay Books/Little, Brown & Co., 1994), 521.
3. Ibid., 522–23.
4. Michelle Newell, MPP, and Jorja Leap, PhD, *Reforming the Nation's Largest Juvenile Justice System: Policy Brief* (Los Angeles: UCLA Luskin School of Public Affairs and Children's Defense Fund-California, 2013).
5. Daniel Beekman, "Bronx's Notorious Spofford, aka Bridges Juvenile Center, Finally Shut Down," *Daily News*, March 31, 2011, http://www.nydailynews

.com/new-york/bronx/bronx-notorious-spofford-aka-bridges-juvenile-center
-finally-shut-article-1.119333.

6. Shane Claiborne, *The Irresistible Revolution: Living as an Ordinary Radical* (Nashville: Zondervan, 2006), 232–37. Taken from *The Irresistible Revolution* by Shane Claiborne Copyright © 2006 by The Simple Way. Used by permission of Zondervan. www.zondervan.com.

Chapter 8: Confusion in the Valley of Vision

1. John Jolliffe, ed. and trans., *Froissart's Chronicles* (London: Faber & Faber Ltd., 2012), Kindle edition.
2. Ibid.
3. Joan Vita Miller and Gary Marotta, *Rodin: The B. Gerald Cantor Collection* (New York: Metropolitan Museum of Art, 1986), 69.
4. Ibid., 44.
5. John L. Tancock, *The Sculpture of Auguste Rodin: The Collection of the Rodin Museum Philadelphia* (Philadelphia: Philadelphia Museum of Art, 1976), 385.
6. Vincent Harding, *Martin Luther King: The Inconvenient Hero* (Maryknoll, NY: Orbis Books, 2008), 3.
7. Johanna W. H. van Wijk-Bos, *Reformed and Feminist: A Challenge to the Church* (Louisville, KY: Westminster John Knox Press, 1991), 13.
8. Ibid.
9. Ibid., 15.
10. Ibid.
11. Abba Antony quoted in *The Paradise of the Desert Fathers*, cited at http://www.thenazareneway.org/paradise-of-the-desert-fathers-htm, spirituality.ucanews.com/2014/12/07/the-paradise-of-the-desert, and elsewhere.

Chapter 9: Parables of Persistence

1. Sojourner Truth, *The Narrative of Sojourner Truth*, dictated by Sojourner Truth, ed. Olive Gilbert (Boston: The Author, 1850), http://www.digital.library.upenn.edu/women/truth/1850/1850.html. All subsequent quotes by Sojourner Truth were taken from this online source.
2. Kerry Kennedy Cuomo, *Speak Truth to Power: Human Rights Defenders Who Are Changing Our World*, Umbrage Editions (New York: Crown Publishers, 2000), 198.
3. Ibid.
4. Ibid., 199.

Chapter 10: Vigilance

1. "Harriet Tubman: The 'Moses' of Her People," *Christianity Today*, http://www.christianitytoday.com/ch/131christians/activists/tubman.html.
2. "Harriet Tubman (c. 1820–1913)," *Africans in America: Judgment Day*, PBS www.pbs.org/wgbh/aia/part4/4p1535.html.

3. Ibid.
4. Ibid.
5. "Tubman: The 'Moses' of Her People."
6. "Ida Wells (1862-1931)," *American Experience*, PBS, http://www.pbs.org /wgbh/amex/chicago/peopleevents/p_wells.html, accessed February 17, 2016.
7. Ida Wells-Barnett, *The Southern Horrors: Lynch Law in All Its Phases*, 1892, www.gutenberg.org/files/14975/14975-h/14975-h.ht.
8. W. E. B. DuBois, "The Vigilance Committee: A Call to Arms," *The Crisis*, vol. 6, no.1. (May 1913): 26–27.
9. Ibid.
10. Ibid.
11. Ibid.

Chapter 11: Shepherd for the Lost

1. John F. Burns, "Stricken Blind, Solo Pilot Is Guided to Safety," *New York Times*, November 8, 2008, http://www.nytimes.com/2008/11/08/world /europe /08pilot.html?_r=0.
2. Bishop Sally Dyck, "Foreword," in *Weaving a Just Future for Children: An Advocacy Guide*, by Diane C. Olson and Laura Dean F. Friedrich (Nashville: Discipleship Resources, 2008), 11.
3. James Sterngold, "Mountain Lion Attacks Kill 1, Injure 1/Orange County Bicyclists Rescue Woman Victim," *SF Gate*, January 10, 2004, http://www .sfgate.com/news/article/Mountain-lion-attacks-kill-1-injure-1-Orange -2814215.php.
4. Carl Hoffman, "Welcome to the Neighborhood," *Adventure*, October 2004, www-t.nationalgeographic.com/adventure/0410/excerpt5.html, accessed July 4, 2016.
5. Ibid.
6. Ibid.

Chapter 12: Godspeed

1. David L. Liebman, ed., *Etz Hayim: Torah and Commentary* (New York: Rabbinical Assembly, United Synagogue of Conservative Judaism, 2004), 1088–89.
2. Dr. Martin Luther King Jr., "A Time to Break Silence," in *A Testament of Hope: The Essential Writings and Speeches of Martin Luther King, Jr.*, ed. James Melvin (New York: HarperOne, 1991), 243.
3. Phil Gast, "Good Samaritan Describes Chase that Led to Girl's Freedom," CNN, October 7, 2010, http://www.cnn.com/2010/CRIME/10/06/california .child.samaritan/index.html.
4. From "Man Who Saved Abducted Child Says He Was 'Beyond Fear,'" Oct. 6, 2010, Today.com, www.today.com/id/39533885/ns/today-today_news/t /man-who-saved-abducted-child-says-he-was-beyond-fear/#.V3qeTaDDtA,

accessed July 4, 2016, and Naimah Jabali-Nash, "Victor Perez Hailed as Hero for Rescue of Abducted 8-Year-Old Calif. Girl," CBS News, October 8, 2010, http://www.cbsnews.com/news/victor-perez-hailed-as-hero-for-rescue-of-abducted-8-year-old-calif-girl/.

5. Today.com, "Man Who Saved Abducted Child."
6. CBS News, "Abducted Girl's Hero Describes Car Chase Rescue," CBS News, October 6, 2010, http://www.cbsnews.com/news/abducted-girls-hero-describes-car-chase-rescue/.
7. Julia Cass, "The McKee Family," in *Children of Hard Times*, Children's Defense Fund, http://www.childrensdefense.org/policy/endingchildpoverty/children-of-hard-times/Children-of-Hard-Times.html.

Resources for Faithful Child Advocacy from the Children's Defense Fund

1. The material in this section was drawn from the website of the Children's Defense Fund, http://www.childrensdefense.org.